REFLECTIONS IN A
JAUNDICED EYE

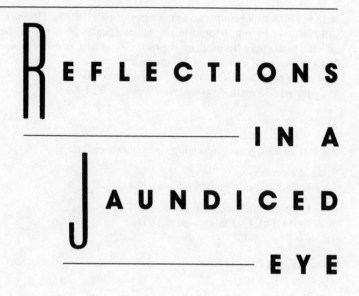

REFLECTIONS IN A JAUNDICED EYE

FLORENCE
KING

ST. MARTIN'S PRESS
NEW YORK

Design by Jaye Zimet

Library of Congress Cataloging-in-Publication Data

King, Florence.
    Reflections in a jaundiced eye.

    1. American wit and humor.   I. Title.
PS3561.I4754R4   1989   818'.5407   88-29810
ISBN 0-312-02646-3

First Edition
10 9 8 7 6 5 4 3 2 1

To the memory of my mother,

Louise Ruding King

CONTENTS

REFLECTIONS IN A
JAUNDICED EYE

1

AUTHOR'S NOTE

If suicide notes can be said to possess nationality, surely the most American one was left by historian Wilbur J. Cash: "I can't stand it anymore, and I don't even know what *it* is."

In 1964, rightwing maven Phyllis Schlafly published a book called *A Choice, Not an Echo* in which she condemned President Lyndon B. Johnson for awarding the Medal of Freedom to the leftwing literary critic Edmund Wilson. Among her objections to Wilson, Schlafly noted: "Edmund Wilson revealed his lack of patriotism in these words from his latest book (*The Cold War and the Income Tax*): 'I have finally come to feel that this country, whether or not I continue to live in it, is no longer any place for me.'"

It's time Schlafly knew that Alexander Hamilton said it first. In a letter to Governor Clinton of New York he wrote: "Every day proves to me more and more that this American world was not made for me." Moreover, in another letter to Rufus King, Hamilton said: "Am I a fool— a romantic Quixote—or is there a constitutional defect in the American mind?"

Like all members of the God 'n' Country Club, Schlafly

thinks that only leftwing teeth are set on edge by America. She's wrong. I'm slightly to the right of Baby Doc, but life in America has the same effect on me as "The Morton Downey, Jr. Show."

Alexander Hamilton was neither a fool nor a romantic Quixote. According to the laws of logic, A is A; a thing cannot be other than itself; parallel lines cannot meet. Except in America, where the movement of Birnam Wood to Dunsinane is a regular occurrence in the lumberyard of our national psyche. Unstrung Americans are found in both political camps, and our common motto is: "My nerves, right or wrong."

This book is about my nerves and the lumberyard. That's not a good title, however, so I called it *Reflections in a Jaundiced Eye.*

2 CONFESSIONS OF A BLOOM & HIRSCH GIRL

In the summer of 1987 millions of Americans devoured two nonbeach books, *Cultural Literacy* by E.D. Hirsch and *The Closing of the American Mind* by Allan Bloom. You know what that means. We are in for a fad of massive proportions. Culture is in the Green Room, practicing its sound bites while waiting to take a whack at our gross national attention span.

I was a Bloom & Hirsch girl before Bloom & Hirsch were cool. It all started in Washington, D.C. in 1940. At four, I was at that familiar stage when children discover scissors and cut out pictures from newspapers and magazines. Like all kids in the throes of this craze, my preferences were eclectic—a racehorse from the sports page, a Jiggs and Maggie comic strip, a dictator on a balcony—until our long-suffering family doctor gave me sudden direction.

3

Unwrapping his blood pressure cuff from my grand-mother's arm, he signaled my parents into the kitchen. I followed and listened to the verdict.

"I won't be responsible if she doesn't stop reading that column," he warned. "They're *all* on the verge of a stroke. I treated three of them last week."

"They" were Granny's cronies in the Daughters, and "that column" was *My Day* by Eleanor Roosevelt.

Granny's political opinions defied the entire body of Western rational thought—*i.e.*, she was a Southern Democrat. To her way of thinking, Franklin Delano Roosevelt could do no wrong except when he did something wrong, and since that could not happen, someone else must have done it.

She knew perfectly well who that someone was. *That woman* made Mr. Roosevelt invent Social Security because she was a Socialist. *That woman* made Mr. Roosevelt recognize Russia because she was a Communist. The colored were forgetting their place because *that woman* was stirring them up. Lazy actors were being paid good money to put on Federal Theater plays because *that woman* was planting secret messages.

If the subject was over her head, like the gold standard, she issued her all-purpose explanation.

"That woman drugged him."

Each day that Mrs. Roosevelt's column ran in the *Washington Daily News*, Granny watched at the window for the delivery boy and made a beeline for the paper when she heard the thump at the door. She always turned directly to the fatal page. Soon she started turning red. By the time she got to the end of the first paragraph, the faint pink birthmark between her eyebrows had darkened until it burned like a scarlet brand. As she read on, she turned lethally glorious shades of maroon, magenta, and vermilion, just like the contents of my Crayola box. Her bosom, which would have put Dolly Parton to shame, heaved like multitudinous waterwings incarnadined as the flush spread down her neck and chest, which were one and the same.

When she could stand no more, she dropped the paper and emitted a strangled cry.

"Bring me my digitalis!"

After the doctor's ultimatum, my parents discussed the problem. Herb, my British father and the only intellectual in our family of pseudo-genteel Yahoos, came up with a solution calculated to save his mother-in-law's life and give me a head start on reading.

"Florence likes to cut things out of the paper," he said. "Let her cut out Mrs. Roosevelt's column before Mrs. Ruding sees it."

Granny reluctantly agreed, and censorship became my first household chore. I got into it in a big way. I had just seen one of those crusading newspaper movies starring James Gleason as the tough-talking editor who slashed at copy while wearing a green eyeshade. I fell in love with the idea of the eyeshade, so Herb bought me one to wear while I slashed Mrs. Roosevelt. Several afternoons each week, while Kate Smith belted out "God Bless America" on the radio, I sat in our grim, windowless kitchen ell (which I called my "ministry" after seeing another movie) and rolled back constitutional guarantees.

I had no trouble finding Mrs. Roosevelt's column because her picture was on it. Soon, though, encouraged by Herb, I began noticing other things. Often the lead sentence was one she had made famous: *My day has been a most interesting one.* It was the punchline of countless Eleanor jokes I had heard at family gatherings, delivered in imitation of her high-pitched, singsong voice.

Herb had already taught me the alphabet, so he challenged me to sound out the letters. To our mutual delight, I managed to decode the sentence all by myself.

"Let's try another," he said, leaning over my shoulder. "Here's one. 'I weep for the colored people.' You know *I*. Now, *weep*. *W* is wuh-wuh, *e* is eee-eee, *p* is puh-puh."

A few minutes later, everything except the diphthong in *people* made sense to me. I could not contain my triumph.

"I weep for the colored people!"

"Bring me my digitalis!"

My career as the Littlest Censor ended the day Granny suffered another seizure while bending over the waste basket to sneak out the discarded clippings. After that, we decided it was the better part of wisdom to let her read the column.

My tomboy mother never read anything except the sports page, but she gave me a memorable spelling lesson one night as we listened to the radio. When the European news came on, the announcer repeated one word so many times that I could see it in my mind.

"I know how to spell Jew," I said. "J-U."

"No," said Mama. "It's J-E-W."

It was too much for my fledgling hubris. "It can't be!" I protested.

"Well, it is. It's like *few* and *new*."

"I want it to be J-U."

"Tough shit," said Mama. Like Phyllis Schlafly, she taught her young at home.

By the time I started school I could read. I don't remember how or when it happened; it was a gradual process more like digestion than an intellectual endeavor, and just as natural to my way of thinking. When I encountered a new word, the phonic juices flowed over it until it passed through my eyes and emerged from my brain fully formed.

Showing up at school already able to read is like showing up at the undertaker's already embalmed: people start worrying about being put out of their jobs. America's most dedicated enemies of culture are the Education majors who dominate our public elementary schools. In *Looking for Mr. Goodbar*, Judith Rossner identified Ed majors as the college students who always ask, "Is this going to be on the exam?" whenever the professor goes off on an interesting tangent. Brain-dead themselves, their goal is to keep children as dumb as possible for as long as possible so they can get a raise for taking "Principles and Practices of Remedial Education" in summer school.

My first-grade teacher, a classic example of the breed, got mad when I used the word *prostration*—I got it off the label of one of Granny's snake-oil tonics—and sent a note home about the dangers of precociousness to peer group adjustment.

Family reaction was mixed. My stalwart champion was Herb, the only bona fide male feminist I have ever known. Mama was neutral, yet in an odd way on my side. As an unfeminine Southern woman, she had endured so much disapproval herself that she supported any offbeat behavior. Her motto was "Do what you goddamn please," even if it was something sissy like reading.

My cross to bear was Granny, who harbored both an American dread of intellectuals and a Southern dread of female intellectuals.

"If you keep reading, your eyes will fall out and go plop at your feet. They'll just go *plop*! You'll have to stand on the corner with a white cane and a little tin cup, and everybody will say 'There's the poor little blind girl who wouldn't listen to her grandmother.'"

Whenever she caught me reading the *National Geographic* she said, "East, west, home's best." Whenever Herb and I played our version of Scrabble—seeing how many words we could get out of *disestablishmentarianism* or *Constantinople*—she warned us of our likely fate.

"I used to know somebody who made lists all the time. Poor soul, they had to put her away."

The first time I skipped a grade, she was so upset that she even did a little reading of her own to marshal evidence against it.

"I saw in the *Reader's Digest* about a little boy who went to Harvard at thirteen. Brilliant though he was, being around all those older boys and not having any friends his own age made him get downright peculiar. He's a famous professor today, but he wears his clothes inside out and won't have a lamp in his house. He reads beside a jar full of lightning bugs."

The article inspired her "brilliant but not very bright" theory. The more brilliant you were, the more trouble you had performing ordinary, everyday tasks like crossing the street or changing a razor blade. When she caught me peeling potatoes toward me, she cried "Brilliant but not very bright!" with such fervor that I jumped and cut myself, thereby proving her point.

But that wasn't all. The more brilliant you were, the more closely you had to be "watched," and if you got really brilliant, you would have to be "put away." Every Saturday when we drove over to Stephenson's pie factory in Anacostia, she pointed to the redbrick pile of St. Elizabeth's mental hospital and said, "That's where they keep the brilliant people."

This attitude is conventional wisdom in America. We will never have a nation of cultured and reflective citizens as long as the press keeps printing that cautionary sentence: "Neighbors described the gunman as a quiet man who kept himself to himself."

A seafaring movie inspired my first dip into adult literature. *Reap the Wild Wind* had everything, including the interruption of a deep-sea dive by a giant squid. Constructed by Cecil B. DeMille from enough rubber to win the war, it was bright pink with malignant, unblinking black eyes and a talent for making riveting entrances. Suddenly

8

the sunken ship cracked open and there was the squid in all its tentacled glory.

"Here comes Mrs. Ruding," Herb whispered.

I asked him to get the book for me at the adult library. As it turned out, it was not a book but a long short story by Thelma Strabel that had appeared in the *Saturday Evening Post*. He looked up the back issue and we both read it.

In the 3A I read *Kings Row*, which an Ed-major teacher confiscated when I made the mistake of taking it to school and reading it during recess. I was also charged with occupying a swing without swinging. She sent a letter home, the third that semester.

"She's spelled *precocious* wrong again," said Herb.

"She can read what she goddamn pleases," said Mama.

"She's going to be just like that crazy professor who went to Harvard at thirteen," said Granny. "Next thing we know, she'll be running around with a butterfly net."

"It was fireflies, I believe," Herb corrected.

I got rid of the Ed-major teacher when our traditionalist principal took my side in the dispute and skipped me into 3B. I loved my new teacher. When I began to love school as well, Granny, upset over the second skip, exchanged mere nagging for outright terror.

Each morning when she walked me to the door, she told me to watch out for cars with diplomatic tags—an old Washington warning—and described in lurid detail the special dangers they presented to scholars.

"Diplomats always run over little children walking to school," she said. "They're always around early in the morning because they stay up all night at embassy parties. They'll squish you flat until there's nothing left of you except a little grease spot, but they'll never get arrested for it because the police can't touch them."

She waited for me to whine "I don't wanna go to

school," but I never did. Given all my peer problems, I wanted to study even harder so I could grow up to be a diplomat.

I looked forward to junior high. Having a different teacher for each subject, instead of one teacher all day long for a whole semester, would spread the risk of that elementary school game of American roulette wherein the loaded chamber contained an Ed major who hated bookworms.

Having gym instead of recess would reduce the Christians versus Lions aspect of what Ed majors called "Principles and Practices of Playground Dynamics." I didn't expect to enjoy gym but at least it was a *class*, and having heard that you got extra credit for having a clean gym suit, I figured I could wash and iron my way to a passing grade.

Best of all, people said that junior high "fostered maturity," so I figured I was headed for bookworm heaven.

"God, it's just the most fun!" said the girl I sat next to in homeroom. "It's almost like not being in school at all, the way you can get up and go somewhere else every forty-five minutes. The bells at the end of each period are something to look forward to, and the five minutes between classes really help to break up the day. You can go out in the hall and scream your head off!"

If being a bookworm in elementary school was bad, it was fatal in junior high. "Fostered maturity" turned out to be a Head Start program for femininity. Suddenly we could wear lipstick without being sent to the principal's office, and from there everything went down the drain—literally. The only thing most of the girls wanted to study was the toilet bowl to see if there was any blood in it. Somebody was always jumping up and down and screaming "I started! I beat you!"

In this atmosphere I soon exchanged my mark of Zorro for a mark of Cain. The teachers were fine; this time my problem was other girls. Girls were supposed to play dumb for the boys but I, used to Herb, didn't do it. Each time I gave a correct answer in class, the Fostered Maturity clique reacted with the panicky fury of patriots confronted by a traitor. In the cafeteria they had no trouble reciting the wives of Tommy Manville and Artie Shaw, but when I recited the wives of Henry VIII in history class, they turned around and made faces and gagging sounds at me.

As usual, I compounded my problems by taking refuge in books, specifically the Modern Library series. When I told Mama that *Crime and Punishment* was a detective story, she looked dubiously at the jacket.

"He ought to change his name to Ted Dost."

Next came *Fathers and Sons*, followed by *War and Peace*.

"When are you going to get to *Shit and Piss*?" she asked.

I got so deeply into the Russians that I began signing myself "Florence Herbievna." My favorite was Turgenev's *On the Eve*, which contained aspects of interest to Granny. She loved a good terminal illness. Cornel Wilde had just starred in a movie about the life of Frédéric Chopin called *A Song To Remember* and she had gone to see it three times just to watch him spit blood on the piano keys, so I decided to tell her about *On the Eve*.

"It's about a Russian girl named Elena who falls in love with a Bulgarian revolutionary named Insarov, but he has TB."

"She better watch out. You know what they say about men with consumption. When their fever shoots up, it makes them oversexed."

Turgenev must have been raised on the same old wives' tale because that's exactly what happens when Elena visits Insarov in his room.

"He dies in the end, and Elena becomes a nurse in the Crimean War."

"Did she catch another husband?"

"No, ma'am, she didn't want one. Her heart was broken."

"She missed her chance. An army hospital is the best place in the world to look for a husband. Wounded soldiers get a pension."

In college I was an accidental conformist because my tastes just happened to coincide with the wisdom of the hour, which centered around the fifties' husband-hunt.

To avoid wasting energy that could better be spent pursuing their "MrS." degrees, coeds of the Eisenhower years took only those courses in which "all you have to do is read." We were cheered on by the Blooms and Hirsches of the era, who urged female students to acquire a "broad general education" so we could help our husbands get ahead. The idea, like most American ideas, was never thought through, but it had something to do with inviting your husband's boss to dinner and sending him away thinking you were one classy dame.

It's a good thing I never married. My husband's boss would have gone away thinking I was insane because my broad general education included courses like *The English Rural Novel*, which got me into the habit of saying "Eee, by goom, thart's summat." Nor could I resist Flowering Of courses, especially if they were French, which they usually are.

Tragedy 303. The flowering of 17th-century French neoclassical drama. An intensive study of the verse plays of Jean Racine, with special emphasis on *Phèdre*. Friday, 8–11 P.M. Old Storage Building sub-basement. Miss Dalrymple.

That class schedule is an exquisite indication of how Americans really feel about culture. Anyone interested in the finer things in life is presumed to be free on Friday nights from eight to eleven and deserves to be consigned, like Miss Dalrymple, to a root cellar.

Seventeenth-century French drama is called neoclassical because it followed the rules of ancient Greek drama. These are often called "Aristotle's classical unities," but in truth Aristotle can only be blamed for one of them: the unity of *action*, meaning that you can have only one story line with no subplots and no mingling of tragedy and comedy in the hang-loose Shakespearean manner.

Hanging loose was a *non-non* in sevententh-century France. Louis XIV's rigid etiquette was so complicated that a Versailles courtier had to knock on a marquis's door with his index finger and a duke's with his pinkie. This sort of thing was bound to spread to the Crown-supported stage, and it did. To make their task harder, the neoclassical dramatists added two more unities: *place*, meaning that the whole play could have only one set; and *time*, meaning that the events of the story, no matter how titanic and far-reaching, must be compressed into a period not to exceed twenty-four hours—or as we say in America, "Have a good day."

They also expanded Aristotle's dictum on theatrical decorum. He merely said that murder and other violence must not happen onstage, but the neoclassicists, fearful of offending against Versailles-decreed *politesse*, decided that it was bad taste to let anything happen onstage. Instead of showing the action they tell it; the story unfolds in long declamatory speeches hurled at those neoclassical yentas in togas known as "confidants," who serve a threefold purpose: pumping the principals to find out what they're going to do, listening while they tell what they did, and rushing onstage to announce that something has happened.

To impose still more good taste on themselves, the neoclassicists wrote their plays entirely in Alexandrine verse, a rarefied meter that is uniquely tailored to the French language and fits no other. An Alexandrine must have twelve beats and four stresses and it must rhyme with the next line. If it doesn't, the Académie Française will shoot out your kneecaps.

Based on the *Hippolytus* of Euripides, Racine's *Phèdre* (Phaedra) is about an older woman who develops a passion for her stepson. Set in the mythical ancient Greek city of Troezen, the cast is as follows:

> Theseus—King of Athens
> Phèdre—his second wife
> Hippolytus—son of Theseus
> Aricia—a foreign princess
> Oenone—confidante of Phèdre
> Theramenes—confidant of Hippolytus
> Ismene—confidante of Aricia
> Panope—confidante-at-large

Phèdre opens with Hippolytus confiding to his confidant, Theramenes. He says that he has decided to conduct a search for his father, Theseus, who in classic Greek fashion has forgotten to come home from a journey. He adds that he is glad to have an excuse to get away from Troezen at this time because his stepmother, Phèdre, has been inexplicably hostile to him of late, and also because . . . well, something has happened.

The confidant is all ears, so Hippolytus indulges in that Racinian neurotic compulsion known as *"rompre le silence"*—what spies do under torture. He confides that his former immunity to female charms has collapsed and he has fallen in love with Aricia, "that sole survivor of an impious race"—*i.e.*, she's the daughter of the rival political family that tried unsuccessfully to overthrow Theseus and wrest his kingdom from him.

This is a silence that should not have been romped because Aricia is under house arrest. A firm believer in heredity, Theseus decided that her bloodlines were so politically dangerous to him that she must never be allowed to reproduce. Before leaving on his journey, he forbade her to marry, ordered her held hostage in his palace so she couldn't meet any men, and had signs reading *"Défense de Foutre Aricia"* posted in the Troezen metro. The only man he trusts her with is his son, Hippolytus, because it's a well-known fact that *il est chaste*.

Now that Hippolytus has kicked off, the logorrhea shifts into high gear. Enter Oenone, Phèdre's confidante, with word that something has happened: her mistress is dying of *"une maladie secrète."*

Hippolytus and Theramenes exit and Phèdre enters with word that something has happened: her strength has failed, her hair (*cheveux*) has grown heavy, her eyes (*yeux*) have gone bad, her knees have buckled, and she has lost her mind.

Oenone perks up, certain that these titanic afflictions are emotionally based, the result of a world-class secret that Phèdre has kept to herself instead of confiding to her confidante, who would be only too happy to spread it all over Troezen. Referring contemptuously to secret-keeping as *"le silence inhumain,"* she starts pumping.

> Oenone: Aimez-vous?
> Phèdre: De l'amour j'ai toutes les fureurs.
> Oenone: Pour qui?
> Phèdre: J'aime. . . .
> Oenone: Qui?

Phèdre romps the silence and names Hippolytus, then pours out the whole story of her guilty passion in fifty exquisitely rhymed Alexandrines, explaining that she has only pretended to hate her stepson in order to conceal her lust for him.

Suddenly they are interrupted by Panope, a beginning confidante apprenticed to Oenone, who rushes onstage to announce that something has happened: Theseus died on his way home from his journey.

Now that Phèdre is a widow, her guilty passion is no longer guilty. Egged on by Oenone, she decides to tell Hippolytus that she loves him.

But Hippolytus's tongue has also been loosened by the news of his father's death. In the next act we find him declaring his love to Aricia. He wants her, he says, bad blood and all, and she might as well stay and hear him out because *"J'ai commencé de rompre le silence."* When these people start, they can't stop.

Fortunately for Aricia, he is interrupted by his confidant, who tells him that Phèdre wishes to see him. Aricia and Theramenes exit and Phèdre confronts the virginal hunk. But when she declares her passion, the prissy Hippolytus recoils in horror. The scorned Phèdre flees.

As soon as she's gone, Theramenes runs back in to find out what happened, but Hippolytus refuses to tell him, saying *"cet horrible secret"* must remain forever buried. It's the worst thing you can say to a confidant, but the boy is thick.

The next act opens with the scorned Phèdre in a tirade, calling Hippolytus *"Misérable! Détestable! Sauvage! Odieux!"* because the next line ends in *"mes yeux"*.

At this point, Oenone rushes onstage with word that something has happened: Theseus isn't dead after all; that new confidante Panope got it all wrong. He's alive and well and will be home any minute.

Phèdre panics. The puritanical Hippolytus will surely tell his father that she put the make on him. What can she do to protect herself against her husband's certain fury?

Oenone comes up with a damage-control plan, telling

Phèdre that she must get to Theseus first and accuse Hippolytus of rape before he gets a chance to accuse her of attempted adultery. Phèdre, already wracked by guilt, reduces the charge to sexual molestation and Oenone bustles off to tell Theseus all about it.

It's a bad time to approach Theseus because Theramenes has just told him that Hippolytus wants to marry Aricia. When Oenone tells him that the prince tried to rape his stepmother, Theseus bellows *"Perfide! Monstre! Fils criminel! Profane adultère! Lâche incestueux!"* so it will all rhyme with *"les yeux."*

The next scene finds Hippolytus and Aricia making plans to run away together. Worried that someone will find out, she asks him, "Can you keep silent in this mortal danger?" This has to be the silliest question in all literature. Can any of these people keep their mouths shut? No, my leetle cabbage, as soon as your back is turned he will run and tell his confidant every word you said.

Hippolytus exits and Theseus enters to tell Aricia what Oenone told him that Phèdre told her about what Hippolytus did, but she refuses to listen. Nor will she let him pump her about what Ismene heard from Theramenes. She says she intends to flee his presence that very minute because she cannot endure any more gossip, or as Racine puts it: *"Pour n'être pas forcés à rompre le silence."*

Once again Panope rushes onstage with word that something has happened: Oenone has drowned herself. It was, she says, a mad (*furieux*) act that will hide her forever from our eyes (*yeux*). Never mind our ears, they don't rhyme.

While everyone is talking about what happened to Oenone, Theramenes rushes onstage with word that something else has happened: Hippolytus has been killed in a chariot wreck. The bad news is that it was a terrible sight (*affreux, yeux*). The good news is that the mortally wounded prince lived long enough to confide in his confidant one last time.

He used his last breath to tell Theramenes to tell Theseus that nothing happened between him and Phèdre, and to beg his father not to let anything happen to Aricia. (Nothing will as long as she stays on that stage).

While everyone is talking about what happened to Hippolytus, Phèdre staggers in and announces that something has happened to her: she has taken poison, but before she dies she wants to tell everyone what really happened. *"Il faut rompre un injuste silence,"* she begins, and proceeds to clear her stepson's name.

> *"C'est moi qui sur ce fils chaste et respectueux*
> *Osai jeter un oeil profane, incestueux."*

Only one eye this time, she doesn't have much wind left. After she dies, Theseus vows to honor his son's last request, declaring that he will adopt Aricia as his daughter and treat her as a member of the family.

He has to—*fille* rhymes with *famille*.

I graduated from college qualified to do nothing except crossword puzzles in ink. Though a scholarship student, I received an aristocrat's education, designed for people like the ante bellum Ashley Wilkes who have the money and leisure to enjoy it for its own sake. But polished proletarians have to make a living. That's hard to do when employers keep saying you're "overqualified"—or worse, hire you anyway. Nothing is more frustrating than sitting in an office amid typewriters and mimeographers when you know what *deus ex machina* means.

My classmates who went for their MrS. had it worse. Because America regards culture as woman's work, generalist movements in education always contain the seeds of antifeminism. The all-you-have-to-do-is-read brigade formed the backbone of the feminine mystique and bought the aprons inscribed with "For This I Spent Four Years In College?" But they should not have felt as uselessly decorative as they did because they performed a service for America that is sorely missed today.

I refer to what used to be called the "Scarsdale conference," named for advertising men who took work home and laid certain professional problems in the laps of their housebound wives.

American men have always preferred pragmatic curricula, but at least when women went to college to catch husbands they caught a few other things as well. Stuffed full of all those Appreciation Of and Flowering Of courses, coeds of the fifties absorbed, often in spite of themselves, a vast array of cultural miscellany, so that when their copywriter husbands asked their advice, they were able to keep the poor dumb slobs from making the kind of knuckleheaded mistakes so prevalent today.

No husband of the fifties would have named a car "Cressida" because his wife, when she got through laughing, would have recited Shakespeare's *"O Cressid! O false Cressid! False, false, false! Let all untruths stand by thy stainèd name and they'll seem glorious!"* Nor would he have named a motorcycle "Virago" as the Yamaha company did. His wife would have said yes, it does have something to do with *virile*, but it means a quarrelsome, unfeminine woman, a scold; or a strong, manlike woman, an Amazon—in neither case the kind of image young studs wish to project.

Today the liberated daughters of these cultural heroines are marching forth with MBA degrees, proudly competing on an equal footing with MBA-ed males. What they actually are is equally ignorant. If we have already been treated to cars named Cressida and motorcycles named Virago, what else will slip by these dress-for-success nincompoops? If they try to use the enriching information they are going to get from Bloom & Hirsch sound bites, the Land of Hopefully and Glory can look forward to:

"Pyrrhic Victory"—the after-shave for sexual athletes

"Horst Wessel" lunchmeat

"Effluvia" deodorant

"Stonehenge"—the robber-proof door lock

"Annabel Lee" beach togs

"Caveat Emporium" variety stores

"Medea"—the baby carrier for the having-it-all mother

"Lupine" toothpaste for the smile they won't forget

"Shylock"—the body wave for troublesome hair

"Ultima Thule" laxative suppositories

The worst enemy culture ever had is a woman named Bea.

Bea is a fixture in American life and the nemesis of the poor-but-bright kid. Her stamping grounds are the working class, the lower-middle class, and what Southerners prefer to call the shabby-genteel class. Wherever you find six plaster ducks flying across the wall in graduated sizes, there too will you find Bea.

Bea can be your aunt, your mother's cousin, or the neighbor down the hall who becomes a family friend. Usually she's childless, not because she's a spinster but because "she was married for a little while." In plaster duckland this means that her husband of two months went out to buy a pack of cigarettes and never came back. Since then Bea has operated Bea's Beauty Parlor, where she gets even with men by saying "Honey, I know exactly what you mean" a dozen times a day.

The poor-but-bright kid loved the plaster ducks when she was little, especially the baby one that brought up the rear. She loved Bea, too. Bea is the kind of adult that children love because she loves children. She plays "Adam and Eve and Pinch-Me-Tight" very gently, lets you help her clean out her pocketbook, and smells sugary from Woolworth's perfume.

The poor-but-bright kid has no trouble with Bea in elementary school. Bea thinks it's fine to get good grades then, because at that age, scholarly triumphs are linked to unthreatening conventional virtues like obedience, politeness, and in the case of females, docility. Elementary school is also the place where neatness counts, and to Bea's way of thinking, the poor-but-bright kid's perfect notebooks and her own perfect comb-outs are one and the same. It's all a matter of doing your lessons.

The Bea hive starts to stir in high school when curricula fork off into "academic" and "commercial." The poor-but-bright kid gets placed in academic and receives her first Bea sting.

"Say something in French."

Bea has teased you before, but this time the old warmth is missing. Two shiny pinpoints of hostility are visible in her eyes; you sense that you have done something wrong but you don't know what it is.

When college time comes, Bea gives every appearance of enthusiasm and encouragement.

"Don't be like me," she says. "Make something of yourself."

The poor-but-bright kid wins a scholarship and goes to college. Now that lessons have turned into study, Bea makes a point of asking "What are you studying?"

"Anthropology."

"Ann who?"

"Anthropology," the poor-but-bright kid repeats, blushing.

"Lord, I couldn't even pronounce it much less study it."

Bea gets in some of her best stings when the poor-but-bright kid is called on to define something involving confusing concepts and big words that she's afraid to use for fear of seeming to show off, like the Romantic Movement in literature.

"No, it's not romance as in love story, it's . . . it's. . . ."

What? A rebellion against the strictures of classicism? Yes, but you can't say that because it will only get you in deeper. The elevation of emotion over reason? True, but Bea will just say there's nothing like a good cry. A movement launched by Jean-Jacques Rousseau? Fine, but it will trigger a "Who dat?" straight out of Amos 'n' Andy.

What, then, can you say? While you grope for the answer you know so well, Bea's eyes glitter with vengeful pleasure.

"I went to the college of hard knocks myself."

A highlight of the Bea inquisition is the dinnertime discussion of epistemology. I defy any poor-but-bright kid to refrain from mentioning epistemology at the table. You know perfectly well what Bea is going to do with it; handing her a word like that is like handing a child a loaded gun, but by now you can't help it. You are in the grip of compulsion. Bea has filled you with so much free-floating education guilt that you're like those people who walk into the police station and confess to murders they didn't commit.

"What are you studying?"

"Epistemology." See? Out it comes.

"Do *what*?"

"Epistemology." Compulsion strikes again.

"What in the world is that?"

Would you believe a third time? The police would, they're used to this sort of thing.

"Epistemology is the study of knowledge, how we know what we know."

"Is that what your mama and daddy are sending you to college for?"

The "sending" rings like a cash register. Nobody is

22

sending you to college; you won a scholarship, but not a soul at that table remembers it because Bea, with her good ole girl whiskey voice and her warm, down-home manner has planted the idea that you're a lazy dilettante.

It's pointless to try to defend yourself because the defense involves a boast. Utter one word about scholarships and you will receive the ultimate Bea sting.

"You think you're better than everybody else just because you went to college."

There you have her—Bea, the woman behind the other coffee cup who convinces your mother that she scrubbed floors to send you to college, when in actual fact your mother never even scrubbed her own floors.

Bea's magic spell is everywhere. She played a role in the creation of that "effete corps of impudent snobs" who got Spiro Agnew's goat. Many of America's professional esthetes are motivated less by a devotion to the arts than by a murderous determination to get back at Bea, the poor-but-bright kid's anti-Muse. It tends to be a futile battle because she usually wins in the end. Bea-hemians read a lot of books, but just to be absolutely sure they never open one that Bea might have heard of, they skip *Madame Bovary* and read *A Sentimental Education*, skip *Jane Eyre* and read *The Professor*, skip *David Copperfield* and read *Martin Chuzzlewit*, until eventually they end up almost as ignorant as Bea.

Intellectuals with humble origins who go all-out to change their regional accents often have a Bea in their bonnets. The most Bea-set individual I've ever known was a woman I met at the University of Mississippi thirty years ago. Born in Appalachia, she first sought escape from Bea-attitudes by painting over her mountain twang with the chewy lingua malaria of the aristocratic South Carolina low country. Just when she was beginning to sound like Gullah Jack, the civil rights movement came along and made being a Southerner unfashionable. She responded by rolling back both of her accents and adopting enlightened Boston Kennedy pronunciations. Meanwhile, like so many of our Bea-stung intellectuals, she did not want to sound too American, so she stirred in some BBC and imitated Churchill's lisp. When she combined all of this with her avant-garde commitment to obscenity, "cocksucker" took on new meaning.

Bea is one cause of elitism in the media, for the simple reason that media people usually major in subjects that she can get a handle on. She's incapable of twitting physicists and mathematicians, but literature, history, political science, and journalism are general enough to give her a toe in the door. The supercilious sneers emanating from America's television screens and editorial pages are frequently triggered by the successful poor-but-bright kid's remembrance of things pissed.

If the masses object to media elitism they could end it very quickly by abandoning their contradictory American game of worshipping education while simultaneously hating the educated, but they show no signs of doing so. The plaster ducks are gone now, replaced by oil paintings of deer on black velvet, but life in the poor-but-bright kid class still sucks.

3

GOOD KING HEROD

One night after a lecture, a woman asked Ambrose Bierce for some advice on rearing children. He replied, "Study Herod, madam, study Herod."

My aversion to children took root the day I started kindergarten in 1941, but it didn't flower until a few weeks later when something else happened.

Shortly before Thanksgiving, Granny's Aunt Cora Whittaker died at the age of ninety-four. It was fitting that she went when she did because she considered Thanksgiving a Yankee holiday and had always observed it with a sickroom menu of boiled eggs and junket.

The day before her death she summoned me to her bedside and reached painfully under her pillow with purplish arthritic fingers.

"I want you to have this," she said in a labored whisper.

It was a miniature Egyptian mummy case. Inside was a tiny enameled pharaoh holding crossed canes on his chest.

"It's a pendant," she explained. "You can wear it on a chain when you grow up. Mr. Whittaker gave it to me. He bought it at the World's Fair the year that woman named Little Egypt did the belly dance."

Aunt Cora's was the first death I ever experienced and I felt it deeply. She and I had taken warmly to each other during our brief time together on earth. She had entertained me with stories about the Civil War, which she called "the War of Northern Aggression," describing in vivid detail her memories of watching the battle of Bull Run from atop a barn on her father's farm.

For the next several weeks, I watched a war of my own making unfold in my mind. I was haunted by an irrational fear that one of my kindergarten classmates would steal my mummy—irrational indeed, because I never took it to school. At Herb's suggestion, I had given it to him for safekeeping and he had put it in his strongbox.

Still, the fantasy surged on, battering me with red cyclones of interior rage. Soon it was not just one thief but all of my classmates in a conspiracy to hide the mummy so I would never find it. I imagined grinning child faces, grubby child fists held out tauntingly, piping child voices saying "Pick one." I committed mental mass murder—choking, beating, stabbing children until I got my mummy back.

This reasonless fury started me on my lifelong habit of grinding my teeth in my sleep.

"What's that?" said Granny from her side of the convertible sofa we shared. "I swear, there's a mouse in the wall."

When she realized it was me, it kicked off a long, rambling seminar that was neither dental nor psychiatric but entirely genealogical in the best Southern manner, participated in by all of our relatives, most of our neighbors, and several Daughters from Granny's chapter.

Does teeth-grinding run in our family? No. What about Augustus Fairbanks who smiled with his gums? No, Augustus just had stubby teeth. He got them from his mother.

26

She was a Wheeler—all the Wheelers have stubby teeth. Wait! You remember Olive Upton whose ears closed up? They say it had something to do with her jaw bone. Yes, but Olive was adopted so there's no blood there. *Then why is the child grinding her teeth?*

To Granny, if it wasn't a family trait, I wasn't really doing it.

"It's all in your mind," she said, with more truth than she knew.

"No, it isn't. I do it because I'm mad at *them*," I blurted.

Mama turned around from the front seat of the car. "Who?"

I hadn't planned to tell them about my private war, but it was too late now. I hesitated, gazing out the car window at the red mud of Montgomery County. It was Sunday; in keeping with the de rigueur custom of pre-World War II Washington, we were taking a pleasure drive through the Maryland countryside.

"The kids at school," I said at last. "I'm afraid they'll steal Aunt Cora's mummy."

Herb looked at me in the rearview mirror.

"That's in my strongbox."

"I know, but suppose it wasn't?" My voice began to tremble. "Suppose I took it to school?"

"Suppose one thing, suppose another, suppose a monkey was your brother?" Granny singsonged.

"But if—"

" 'If you can keep your head while all about you are losing theirs,' da-dum-da-dum. . . . How does the rest of that go?"

The chapbook hour came to an abrupt end. Suddenly there was a heavy thud from the rear of the car, followed by a dragging sound. I looked out the back window and saw a long piece of rusty pipe lying in the middle of the road.

"The bloody drive shaft fell off!" Herb yelled.

He coasted over to the muddy shoulder and went to retrieve our transmission system. A few minutes later a farmer came along in a truck and promised to send somebody back to tow us. We settled in to wait.

"Might as well listen to the radio," said Mama, reaching for the knob.

"*. . . bombed Pearl Harbor shortly after seven* A.M. *Hawaiian time. . . .*"

See? I told you there was a war going on. Granny inadvertently kept things perking along with her Gay Nineties songs. When she wasn't singing about fallen women, she was singing about children in extremis or worse. My favorite was "The Snowy Night." When I sang it on Sing Me a Song Day in first grade the teacher sent a note home.

> *Just then the church door opened,*
> *The wedding guests turned 'round.*
> *And seeing the intruder,*
> *They dared not make a sound.*
> *"Stop!" the ragged woman cried,*
> *"My story must be told!*
> *The bridegroom is the father*
> *Of this dead child that I hold!"*

The situation heated up when I read *Gone With the Wind* at the age of eight. Granny laid low for once, obviously hoping that it would inspire me to stop reading altogether and become the Southern belle she wanted me to be. She refrained from saying "Get your nose out of that book!" and waited for me to identify with Scarlett.

I identified with the Tarleton twins—both of them. It turned into an obsession. I read the scenes in which they appeared over and over until I could recite them by heart. I spun long plotless fantasies of them dressed in gold-braided gray uniforms and sitting together on the steps of

Tara—without Scarlett. I ached to see what they "really" looked like. I had seen the movie at the age of four but remembered nothing of it except the burning of Atlanta and the horse dying in the traces. In effect, I had "missed" the movie, as we said in pre-VCR days, and there were as yet no plans to re-issue it. I lived with a dull sense of miserable certainty that I would never see it, never see *them*.

Literal-minded Granny assumed that my Tarleton mania was a desire for siblings.

"Do you want twin brothers?"

"No, ma'am."

"Do you want twin sisters?"

"No, ma'am."

"Do you want one brother?"

"No, ma'am."

"Do you want one sister?"

"No, ma'am."

"You're so selfish."

She was so right. I wanted no interference with my only child's balance of power.

Her next interpretation was exquisitely in character. She decided that I was becoming precocious in the correct Southern way and wanted Stuart and Brent Tarleton for my beaux.

"I knew a girl who had two brothers in love with her. They shot each other." She sighed fondly.

Next to genealogy, Granny's favorite subject was gynecology, so one way or another she was always talking about blood. When it finally dawned on her that I wanted to *be* the Tarleton twins—both of them—she banished the psychological aspects of the case with a wave of her wand and pulled a gynecological rabbit out of the hat.

"You know," she said pensively, "your mother had two waters when you were born. The first one broke very early.

We thought you were coming then, but you didn't. Then, about three hours later, the second one broke and you were born."

She gazed off into space, her voice taking on the oh-the-aching-wonder-of-it-all note that always accompanied her old wives' tales.

"They say a baby can start out to be twins, but if one baby is strong and the other is weak, something terrible happens."

"What?" I asked.

The upshot of her theory was that I had committed murder in utero. A Darwinist at heart despite her good works, she believed that I, the stronger of the two fetuses, had overpowered my weaker wombmate, consumed all the available nourishment, and finally devoured my wombmate in my struggle for existence.

"That's why some people have a fingernail or a tiny sliver of bone embedded in a mole," she concluded. "That's all that's left of the poor little baby they ate."

Thereafter, I examined my moles with maniacal scrutiny, and I am still an inveterate picker of scabs. As the yuppie said when he skipped the sex scenes in the steamy novel about Wall Street entrepreneurs: "I want to get to the good parts."

America is not a democracy, it's an absolute monarchy ruled by King Kid. In a nation of immigrants, the child is automatically more of an American than his parents. Except in families that go back so far it no longer matters, Americans regard children as what Mr. Hudson in "Upstairs, Downstairs" called "betters."

Aping their betters, American adults do their best to turn themselves into children. Puerility exercises *droit du seigneur* everywhere. Television weather reporters affect guess-what tones and breathless gasps while pointing at cartoons of sad-faced clouds. Naughty allusions to "the F word" have inspired infantile discussions of taxes (the T word), liberals (the L word), and race (the R word). On Halloween, some hospitals station costumed technicians in emergency rooms to X-ray candy to make sure nobody murders the little wartlings with tricky treats.

"Precious Cargo Aboard" signs decorate car windows and LOV KIDS vanity plates bring up the rear. Like Nero, who couldn't sing but sang anyway, kiddie artists get their smeary creations framed and hung on the walls of public buildings and medical clinics, and more and more novels are being written in the present tense because "he fucks her hard . . . she moans and writhes" is the way children would say it if they did it. We tolerate inarticulateness because it's the adult's way of hanging on to goo-goo; the only time we say what we mean is in commercials that imitate playground contentiousness. The coffee couple yah-yahs their way through "it's rich . . . it's mild . . . it's rich . . . it's mild," while the budget-motel couple chimes in with "price . . . style . . . price . . . style."

European men wax sentimental over older women but the American man dwells lugubriously on kids in telethons that go on for twenty hours; we get tributes to kids, songs about kids, stories about kids, and of course, kids—in person! Liberals take up mess-making politics and conservatives trade McGuffey's Readers like baseball cards. Hostage relatives like Mrs. Barbara Timm, mother of Iranian embassy Marine Kevin Hermening, practice do-it-yourself diplomacy in defiance of government travel bans out of an unshakable belief in the power of personal appeal—the power of the cinematic cute kid whose "Please, mister" melts hearts of Lewis Stone.

A few years ago, Meg Greenfield wrote a column about the "Lesson Syndrome"—the lesson of Vietnam, the lesson of Watergate, and so forth. Since then the blackboarding of America has grown even more intense. Whenever the president or some other public official is au courant, we say "he's done his homework." Moderators ask guest pundits, "What grade would you give the President?" and the pundits bestow approval with, "He deserves high marks."

Picketers and protesters throw themselves down like spoiled children holding their breath, refusing to move and going limp so that police must carry them to the vans. Single-issue politics is coming more and more to resemble the one-track mindedness of children, and their intensely partisan lapel buttons bear scurrilous messages about the opposition that are not far removed from recess battle cries of "Johnny eats worms!"

Antiwar protesters of the sixties chanted "Hey, hey, LBJ, how many kids did you kill today?" as if adult deaths didn't matter. The same contempt for adults cropped up in the Senate hearings on toxic waste some years ago when a New Jersey father broke down and sobbed, "I am thirty-three years old. I don't care what happens to me in the future. But I have two children. Are they going to live?" Only thirty-three, and he doesn't care what happens to himself? Even Edward Kennedy looked shocked.

Our long love affair with the Shirley Temple movie in which the moppet solves all the adult problems and resolves the plot has given us the spectacle of the snotnose as expert witness. The Senate Subcommittee on Child and Human Development observed Save the Children Day by listening to wartlings from all over the country who "came armed with foreign policy strategy and counsel for presidential candidates," said the AP, adding: "Dumped on the table were two mail bags containing 16,000 letters from children."

They've moved in on the Supreme Court, too. The July 29, 1981 issue of *Time* noted: "A year and a half ago, Supreme Court Justice Potter Stewart received a letter from a high school student in St. Cloud, Minn. The Justice had done well, wrote the young woman, but why had he stayed on the job so long?" Stewart, who was then only sixty-six, told the press: "That sort of started me thinking." Eighteen months later, Stewart resigned. If this story is true, it illustrates the audacity of adolescents who dare offer a Supreme Court Justice unsolicited advice on matters they know nothing about. If it's not true, it illustrates something even worse: the American adult's need and eagerness to pretend to be guided by children.

Our cult of the child is a Protestant cult. Catholics urge children into theological adulthood at age seven, when spiritual responsibility begins with the first confession, but Protestants have no comparable rite of passage. Catholics also have the Virgin Mary and numerous female saints to serve as symbols of perfect purity, but Protestants bumped women from the celestial line-up and dredged up the child to fill the void.

Any hope that America would finally grow up vanished with the rise of fundamentalist Christianity. Fundamentalism, with its born-again regression, its pink-and-gold concept of heaven, its literal-mindedness, its rambunctious good cheer (Pat Robertson smiles and laughs so much while he talks that it's sometimes hard to understand what he's saying), its anti-intellectualism (just close your eyes and let it wash over you), its puerile hymns ("Jesus Wants Me for a Sunbeam"), and its faith healing (Jesus will kiss it and make it well) are made to order for King Kid America. In no other country could the invitation to "Come as a child" ring so sweetly in the national ear.

If we want to regain the respect of the world, we should begin by announcing that children have no business expressing opinions on anything except "Do you have enough room in the toes?" As for me, I'll take cats, those symbols of adultness and chief spreaders of impetigo in sandboxes—every little bit helps.

* * *

Do my precious little readers want to play book review? All right. One, two, three—go!

Asked to judge the prospects of women writers, Leo Stein, brother of Gertrude, replied: "If you can take their minds off their wombs, you can help them to some kind of intellectual development."

It's too late for Mary Gordon. Her maternity is so obsessive that reading *Men and Angels* is like being licked. Although her heroine, Anne Foster, is an art historian, she is such a primitive of the motherhood school that she comes across more bovine than human, and gives off a fetid reek every time she opens her mouth on the subject of her children—which is constantly:

"And to her son she gave much that was important in a mother's love: a steamy, rich affection, redolent of the cave."

"There are my children . . . She could smell their thin high sweat."

"How primitive it was, this love of children; flesh and flesh, bone, blood, connection."

"His hair smelled acrid, overripe, like stored grain: she put her lips to it and got a yeasty taste . . . She kissed her son's damp head . . . it was the strongest love she knew, this mother love, knit up of blood."

"Children's rooms were like the warm, cluttered nests of hibernating rodents."

Mothers like this are why God made military schools, but little Peter is surrounded by a regiment of women. So that her story can pulse on like an uncut umbilical cord, Gordon eliminates paternal interference in the first chapter by sending Anne's husband, Michael, off to France on a year's sabbatical.

Fathers don't count for much in the uterine confines

of Mary Gordon's mind. "How were children attached to their father's bodies, where they had never lived, she wondered? He never saw himself as once the flesh that housed them." The supportive Michael offers to take the kids to Europe with him so Anne can finish writing her art catalogue in peace and quiet, but of course she says no. "She'd felt ill with fear when he suggested it. She could barely explain to him what the prospect of living without her children made her feel: derelict, unfranchised, as if she were sleeping on the street." An apt comparison, in view of the fact that women like this created saloons, hobo jungles, and the French Foreign Legion.

Left alone with a mentally disturbed babysitter named Laura Post, Anne revels in an atmosphere in which emotional choices dominate ethical ones: "She couldn't bear to hurry the children, so she knew she would be late for the appointment Laura had made with the electrician."

Even Gordon's passing comparisons are pedophilic. A gesture by an adult is described as "something one of the children would have done to get attention." A woman of seventy-five is given "a childish look of pure disappointment." Not even the weather report can get out of the womb. "She imagined children at the ocean; it was that kind of morning."

But the most riveting sentence in the entire novel occurs when Anne puts clothes on the corpse of a suicide victim: "As a posture, this was not unfamiliar to her; it was not unlike dressing a sleeping child."

Not surprisingly, Gordon's literary style is frequently labored, even dilated: "She despised that tendency in people, that abdication of responsibility in favor of some totemic theory of the power of proximity."

Her metaphors need high forceps: "Anne exchanged the unhealed fear of her children's danger for the dry, well-formed white bone of justice."

Sometimes they even require an episiotomy: "At the

same time she was riven, a torrent split her, top to bottom, with a violent slice."

And there is a gem of unconscious humor when Anne concentrates on "keeping her fists clenched so she wouldn't strike [the babysitter]." If we didn't already know that Gordon is feminine, we know it now.

Even though Anne's shoulders assume the "stoop of apology," this novel would make a wonderful vehicle for Joan Crawford. She could chant her famous "I'll do anything for those kids, you hear me, anything," and Geraldine Fitzgerald could play the hapless babysitter. As for the male characters, they're such bemused satellites that Wendell Corey could play all of them.

What are we to make of this breeched presentation of female priorities coming on the heels of twenty years of feminism? Come close, darlings, and your maiden Aunt Flossie will whisper something in your ear. Ready?

Women will never be free until Mary Gordon's picture appears on a milk carton. Now get the hell out of here and go play on the freeway.

4 SPINSTERHOOD IS POWERFUL

Step into my time capsule. We are going to pay a visit to the Unfriendly Insurance Company, a downtown monolith whose lobby features marble columns topped with gilded acanthus leaves and a ruggedly institutional concrete floor that smells of disinfectant.

We take a slow Up elevator, passing New Policies, passing Claims, passing Annuities, passing Public Relations, passing everything, until we come to an eyrie marked File Room. Under normal conditions this would be the seraglio of Unfriendly Insurance because it contains four dozen females between the ages of eighteen and twenty-two, but these are not normal conditions as we have come to know them in the glorious eighties.

Opening the file room door, the first thing we hear is a hush. Row after row of occupied desks, wall-to-wall girls, yet not a sound except the rustle of papery industry. Our astonishment increases when we look at the clock on the wall. It is 9:10 A.M., yet not only are all the girls working, they are also fully dressed. No one is in curlers, no one is filing her nails, no one is eating, no one is talking on the phone, and no one is reading the horoscope in the morning paper.

The girls don't even look up as we enter. Theirs is not to reason why, and we are about to meet the reason why.

At one end of the room, raised on a dais, is an old oaken desk at which sits the personage known in the men's room as "the Old Oaken Bucket." On the front of the desk, exactly in the center, is a bronze nameplate so heavy that it looks like the door of a mausoleum. Unlike today's plastic models, it has no provision for sliding out an old name and inserting a new one because it was made in a forge. It has never been necessary to change the name on this nameplate, and it never will be, because it belongs to MISS MACINTYRE.

Miss MacIntyre started working as a file clerk at Unfriendly Insurance the day after she graduated from high school during the administration of William Howard Taft; she has been supervisor of the file room since the second administration of Calvin Coolidge. She has two generic names but neither of them is "career woman." The male executives call her a "company girl," which signifies a distaff measure of devotion who is married to her job. She calls herself a "businesswoman."

Miss MacIntyre lives with her widowed mother, who cooks her breakfast every morning and sends her off to work with a hearty lunch in a brown bag. She arrives at the office fifteen minutes early and is buried in work by the time her charges come in at nine on the dot.

She works all morning without a break and exhibits an awesome immunity to distraction. So do her charges. Miss MacIntyre runs a tight ship; being popular interests her not at all. As the supervisor of a bevy of sweet young things who are marking time until they get married, she knows her first duty is seeing to it that they deliver a full day's work for a full day's pay. Her technique predates company-sponsored workshops in group dynamics; the moment she hears a giggle or a whisper she barks "Girls!" and it stops.

Except for the direst emergencies, her girls are forbidden to make or receive personal phone calls, or to practice what Miss MacIntyre calls "fraternization." What will one day be called sexual harassment is unknown at Unfriendly Insurance, thanks to a highly successful pre-feminist version of consciousness raising: whenever a new male employee indicates a lubricious interest in the file room, one of his seasoned co-workers takes him aside and says, "Watch out for Miss Mac."

At noon Miss MacIntyre unpacks her lunch and eats it at her desk. She does not vanish into the boutique veldt for two hours because Mother makes all her clothes from Butterick patterns. Nor does she take time off for psychotherapy; people who know that an entire organization would collapse without them rarely suffer from a lack of self-esteem.

When she gets home she eats the hot dinner that Mother has ready and waiting. The two of them play gin rummy with neighbors until ten o'clock, when Miss MacIntyre goes to bed and gets her usual good night's sleep.

In her fifty-two years at Unfriendly Insurance, Miss MacIntyre has been late to work only once, the time it snowed twenty inches, and of the nearly one thousand sick leave days she has earned since joining the company, she has used nine. Tardiness and absenteeism—which to her way of thinking include Christmas shopping days and "personal leave"—have no place in her rigid conception of herself as a businesswoman.

Miss MacIntyre had a big crowd for her retirement dinner, but many people came out of duty, and a number of them had privately renamed the occasion "Thank God She's Gone Day." Throughout the meal they swapped horror stories about her ironclad ways, the men speculating about whether she had ever had a sex life and the women shaking their heads and saying "the poor thing."

But then something strange happened. During the presentation of the gift watch, when the company president said "You could set your watch by Miss Mac," people started swallowing hard and blinking back tears. Emotions rose still higher when they presented her with her bronze nameplate mounted on a plaque, and by the time they all stood and sang "Auld Lang Syne" there wasn't a dry eye in the house.

Miss MacIntyre has long since gone to her reward but her legend still lingers down at Unfriendly Insurance (since renamed). Whenever the old-timers see a pregnant career woman doing Lamaze exercises on her desk, somebody always says "I bet Miss Mac is spinning in her grave."

It is typical of America that having invented efficiency apartments, singles bars, Me-ism, Soup-for-One, and That Cosmo Girl, we have dropped *spinster* from the language and consider *old maid* a sexist slur.

I make a point of using both whenever I get a chance. When I fill out forms that ask for my marital status, I skip the printed selections, write in *spinster*, draw a block beside it, and check it. When an aluminum-siding telephone salesman asked to speak to "the man of the house," I said "There isn't any, I'm an old maid," and derived enormous satisfaction from his audible gulp.

I am often accused of being an anti-feminist, and my name is mud at *Ms.* magazine, but in truth my whole life has been a feminist statement. The conflict lies not in my outlook and attitudes but in the definition of feminism that has been foisted on America in the late twentieth century.

When feminism awoke from its long sleep in the sixties, I assumed it would be a movement for careerist spinsters who chose to renounce marriage and motherhood for a life of the mind lived with spartan simplicity and dedicated to professional achievement. What else, after all, could "women's liberation" mean?

I soon found out. In no time, the movement split along two pseudo-feminist fault lines, the Lunatic Fringe and the Lunatic Warp and Woof. The former consisted of Ti-Grace Atkinson, Lesbian separatists, and guerrilla theaters like WITCH and SCUM. The latter consisted of frustrated suburban housewives roused by the melancholy seal barks of Betty Friedan.

To isolate the Lunatic Fringe and make feminism "nice," the Lunatic Warp and Woof took pains to tailor the movement to fit the needs of "mainstream" women—that is, married women. They were losing their minds, said Friedan, because they weren't realizing their potential. Thanks to the marvels of technology, housework was now so easy that it could be done in an hour or two, but married women were still stuck at home because our patriarchal Judeo-Christian heritage denied them access to all the competing, achieving, aggressive, assertive, dress-for-success fun. To this end, when Friedan called a Woman's Strike Day she devised a slogan that had *housewife* written all over it: "Don't Iron While the Strike Is Hot."

Next came the Wombies, who unfurled the banner of anthropology à go-go and combed through history looking for the Great Mother. In *The First Sex*, Elizabeth Gould Davis drained Atlantis and found a prehistoric matriarchy full of wonderfully well-adjusted people who chewed on umbilical cords instead of beef jerky and worshipped the birth bucket instead of the machine. Jane Alpert joined the fray with her "Mother Right" theory, triggering earth mother fantasies and fertility dances in the tofu-and-alfalfa set. Wombie feminists rhapsodized about breastfeeding and natural childbirth, and promoted gynecological self-examinations so that women could see and touch the wondrous reproductive equipment that had ruled the universe before our patriarchal Judeo-Christian heritage spoiled all the affirming, sensing, feeling, nurturing, bonding, burgeoning, moon-and-tides fun.

Wife-and-mother feminism encouraged women to Have It All. As soon as they found out what this cavalier phrase involved, they started complaining like Victorian invalids. The housework that Friedan claimed took only an hour or two was killing them; they were too tired to burgeon, too conflicted to nurture, too busy to bond, too guilty to affirm. They wanted to be able to put their families first without being accused of neglecting their careers, and at the same time, to be able to put their careers first without being accused of neglecting their families.

Always ready with an oxymoron, pseudo-feminists came to the rescue with demands for "caring workplaces"— maternal leave, paternal leave, "massive" government day care, "high quality" on-site corporate day care, flextime, and job sharing so that we could all live the way people used to live 'way back before our patriarchal Judeo-Christian heritage spoiled all the sharing, humanizing, cooperating, partnering, compromising, synthesizing, whelp-and-hoe fun.

Feminism's first duty is to give all women a good name but pseudo-feminism has done the opposite. Countless employers have now discovered that the hand that rocks the cradle rocks the boat; most married women with small children are no use to anybody unless the stock exchange is hiring amok-runners. The ceaseless demands of pseudo-feminists and their arrogant premise that the corporate world exists to provide women with careers regardless of cost and upheaval have caused so much hostility and resentment that sexism and misogyny have been rejuvenated and the phrase "women 'n' children" is running together like "damnyankee."

Instead of trying to harden women as real feminists

should by preaching renunciation and dedication, pseudo-feminists have torn them apart by promoting masculine work while simultaneously condemning masculine work habits. Take, for example, Adrienne Rich: "I want to make it clear that I am *not* saying that in order to write well, or think well, it is necessary to become unavailable to others, or to become a devouring ego. This has been the myth of the masculine artist and thinker; and I repeat, I do not accept it."

Bull, madam, bull. If you really reject it, why not say so simply and briefly, instead of dragging in Nixonian preambles, italics, and "repeats"?

The "myth" of the masculine artist and thinker—or any worker—is not myth but fact and I accept it without question. Its real name is *concentration*, and it is achieved by making oneself unavailable to others. Considering how persistent and thickheaded "others" can be, it is also necessary to become what Rich calls a "devouring ego" and I call a double-barreled bastard.

Mendacious pep talks such as Rich's keep married women in a perpetual state of self-doubt and confusion about priorities and make them resentful and jealous of unencumbered women who have never married. Women are always jealous of something. It used to be legs and bosoms; now it's careers and lifestyles. The New Jealousy is marked by a phrase that I encounter regularly in my fan mail.

"If I could do what you do. . . ."

Write the same page twenty times?

"If I could do what you do. . . ."

Write all day Christmas?

"If I could do what you do. . . ."

Get halfway through a book only to realize that you started too late in dramatic time and the whole thing is turning into a flashback? Anybody who chose that moment to ask "When's dinner?" would get *killed*, ladies, and liberal, compassionate Adrienne Rich knows it. She won't tell you; I just did.

One of the best places to find conflicted Having-It-All career matrons is the publishing world, where the damage they do lives after them under somebody else's name.

Editing requires precise concentration combined with a running memory. If, for example, you cut a paragraph about Mrs. Wiggs of the Cabbage Patch, all subsequent references to Mrs. Wiggs of the Cabbage Patch must also be deleted—known as "following through on the cut." If you notice strange things in your reading material, it's because Mary Marvel stopped what she was doing to follow through on the telephone with the babysitter.

Some Having-It-All careerists are so conflicted that they take refuge in denial, like the pregnant editor who simply went underground for the final trimester without ever telling her writers that she was pregnant. First, she stopped answering her mail. Next, she and her secretary worked out a complex system of creative excuses so that nobody could get her on the phone: she was either in an editorial conference, or a sales meeting, or she had "stepped away from her desk." To make sure nobody got a good look at her, she stopped going to literary cocktail parties and turned down invitations to business lunches so that none of the agents would find out. That boon to Mary Marvel malingering, the annual convention of the American Booksellers Association (she's getting ready to go to ABA, she's at ABA, she's recovering from ABA) luckily coincided with the worst period of her pregnancy, so she was able to string it out for another three weeks.

Just as everybody was about to crack, there came an

ecstatic letter announcing that she had been delivered of a child. The purpose behind all this disruptive secrecy was what I call the "O-lan Syndrome," after Pearl Buck's heroine in *The Good Earth*, who dropped her baby in the birth bucket and went immediately back to work in the rice paddy. The editor wanted to hold herself forth as a Superwoman who could have a baby without—are you ready? —disrupting her career. It didn't wash; the eerie sensation that she had vanished into a cave made it less like *The Good Earth* than *The Blue Lagoon*.

Even when nothing serious goes wrong, the practitioners of Mother's Own feminism can be maddening to work with. Take the editor with a five-year-old son whom she was raising according to the precepts of the "Free Children" section of *Ms.* magazine. She wanted him to imbibe the idea that women have a right to careers, so she took manuscripts home with her and edited them while he watched so he would grow up to respect women as equals. When I got my manuscript back, I found that she had drawn little smile button faces in the margins whenever she came to something she liked, and little sad faces with down-turned mouths and teardrops whenever she came to something she wanted me to change. It was like getting a letter from Patricia Schroeder.

It never stops. I used to think it was safe to work with post-menopausal married women whose children were grown—until I got sidetracked by a lawyer in her late fifties who was two months late with an option contract because she was planning her daughter's wedding. That did it: I told my agent to see to it that I worked with men, spinsters, and childless widows *only*. Pseudo-feminists won't like that one bit, but as Patrick Henry used to say, "If this be treason, then tough titty."

My prejudice (read postjudice) against married women was illustrated to perfection in the September 8, 1986 issue of *Newsweek*. When TWA flight attendants were fired after their unsuccessful strike, Victoria Frankovich, president of the Independent Federation of Flight Attendants, was widely believed to have mismanaged the negotiations with TWA boss Carl Icahn. Frankovich's critics faulted her "for not attending a meeting last summer where both the pilots and the mechanics agreed to Icahn's terms. Instead she presided over her husband's class reunion at their Los Angeles home." *Newsweek* quotes Icahn: "I begged her to come to that meeting. If she had shown up, she could have made a deal."

It sounds enough like the career matron shenanigans I have encountered to be entirely believable. Mrs. Frankovich's decision to play hostess for her husband instead of attending a vital meeting is a workplace version of the notorious social trick that women have traditionally pulled on each other, the trick that every feminist screed and consciousness-raising group for the last twenty-five years has deplored: breaking an engagement with a girlfriend at the last minute when a man calls for a date.

If married women are going to do things like this, a boycott might knock some sense into their heads. Employers who have had all they can stand of wife-and-mother feminism should take a leaf from me and practice preferential hiring of spinsters—on the q.t., of course; one must find ways to get around the strictures of a free country. Think of the advantages: employers would get credit for hiring a woman, yet she would have a lifestyle identical to that of male employees from pre-fathering days. She would arrive at the office with no thoughts of babysitters and day care centers dancing like rancid sugarplums in her head, she could put in as much overtime as needed on the shortest notice, and there would never be any spills or vomit on the brief or manuscript she took home.

If this suggestion catches on, I'll dance at an editor's wedding.

* * *

The reason I can "do what I do" is because I've never married. He travels fastest who travels alone, and that goes double for she. Real feminism is spinsterhood.

It's time America admitted that old maids give all women a good name. Take the matter of credit ratings. During the seventies, "single" became a pejorative; it can mean just about anything and usually does. An old maid and a divorcee with three children to support are both "single," but the financial resemblance ends there. Instead of going to obsessive lengths to help women conceal their marital status under the muzzy blanket of Ms., feminists should have encouraged the inclusion of *spinster* on forms and applications. It would have pulled up women's overall credit rating and eliminated some of the automatic discrimination against them as a group caused by the bill-paying problems of liberated divorcees.

The same point applies to auto insurance rates. Old maids look at the road, not at what Jason did to Debbie's dress. It would be one small step for common sense if insurance companies discriminated in favor of women who do not drive with children in the car. Actuarials being by definition the heart and soul of discrimination, however, our pseudo-feminists have already succeeded in nagging one state, Montana, into adopting a unisex risk-factoring law. The Big Sky now prohibits "discrimination on the basis of sex or marital status in the issuance or operation of insurance policies," according to the November 1987 *Phyllis Schlafly Report*—whose author is even less likely to champion old maids than are the pseudo-feminists.

Even as I write this, I am having a fight with Blue Cross & Blue Shield of Virginia over the astronomical premiums they have been charging me. They have qualified me for "Healthy Virginian" reduced rates, but I told them I would rather have old maid rates and suggested they contemplate Jean-Paul Sartre's observation, "Hell is other people," while they figure my stress risk. If that doesn't work, I will tell them to pay a visit to Old Maid Gardens and contemplate the tombstones.

Susan B. Anthony   1820–1906
Anna Dickinson   1842–1932
Dr. Elizabeth Blackwell   1821–1910
Dr. Mary Olive Hunt   1819–1908
Clara Barton   1821–1912
Dorothea Dix   1802–1886
Sarah Grimké   1792–1873
Mary Moody Emerson   1774–1863
Sarah Fuller   1836–1927
Harriet Smith   1818–1905
Abigail F. Spear   1833–1927
Sarah E. Doyle   1830–1922
Elizabeth Spear   1842–1934
Elizabeth Peabody   1804–1894
Laura Clay   1849–1941
Sarah M. Peale   1800–1895
Elizabeth Sturgiss   1788–1873

A certain teacher and activist is little known today outside feminist history circles, but she is the undisputed star of Old Maid Gardens. Here she is, that perennial unplucked flower of reform politics. . . .

Emily Howland   1827–1929

By God, that's what you call a good set of bowels. Have you ever noticed that there are no old maids in Correctol and Ex-Lax commercials? They beam the message that women are three times more likely than men to suffer from constipation, yet the sufferers portrayed in these minidramas are always matrons and their married daughters, who discuss the problem and conclude that it comes from "doing so much for others"—an unconscious gem of truth-in-advertising hinting that marriage and motherhood are the ties that bind.

Spinsterhood is Nature's Own feminism, the only kind that works, but the vast majority of women would rather explode than admit it. Reviving old maid jokes might help to change their minds. Far from being sexist, as the pseudo-feminists claim, these jokes indicate a much greater degree of real independence than anything enjoyed by today's beset practitioners of Having It All.

Before going to bed, the old maid of song and story spent half an hour locking the doors and windows of a house she occupied alone. It sounds like a big house. She also had plenty of privacy in the asparagus patch where she played leapfrog without benefit of masturbation workshops, so she must have owned a good deal of land as well. Her ability to hire "hired men" was limitless, and when she begged them to marry her she always rattled off a tempting list of livestock to make them forget her lack of physical charms. The "feminization of poverty" is nowhere in evidence in these jokes, whose message is the valuable reminder that emotional deprivation (if such it be) has its compensations.

In my many rereadings of *Gone With the Wind* I never did identify with Scarlett, and the Tarleton twins long ago lost their charm for me. Now my favorite character is India Wilkes:

> The mantle of spinsterhood was definitely on her shoulders now.... Her pale lashless eyes looked directly and uncompromisingly upon the world and her thin lips were ever set in haughty tightness. There was an air of dignity and pride about her now that, oddly enough, became her bet-

ter than the determined girlish sweetness of her days at Twelve Oaks.

As this passage indicates, people like old maids more than they realize. It's especially true of men, who have been brought up to value renunciation for the sake of higher purposes. This bleak male outlook has been condemned by pseudo-feminists, but Richard Lovelace's "I could not love thee, dear, so much, loved I not honour more" is the unhumanized man at his best. Men are not very good at loving, but they are experts at admiring and respecting; the woman who goes after their admiration and respect will often come out better than she who goes after their love.

Of all the benefits of spinsterhood, the greatest is carte blanche. Once a woman is called "that crazy old maid" she can get away with anything.

5 FROM CAPTAIN MARVEL TO CAPTAIN VALIUM

Sometimes I think there is a conspiracy to drive American men insane. The November 30, 1981 issue of *Newsweek* contained a Lifestyle article about the joys of single parenting called "A New Kind of Life With Father," and another called "An Epidemic of Incest"—in the same issue.

During the feminist seventies men were caught between a rock and a hard-on; in the fathering eighties they are caught between good hugs and bad hugs. Any man reading that issue of *Newsweek* would be entirely justified in following the advice in the Camel cigarettes "Where a Man Belongs" ad that shows a drifter, his duffel bag beside him, frantically pumping his way out of town on a railroad handcar in pursuit of the womanless world of vagabondism.

If he did, he would promptly run into the "feminization of poverty." The world of the down-and-out used to be an exclusively masculine society, but now those colorful denizens of male despair, the Bowery bum and the rail-riding hobo, have been replaced by the bag lady and the welfare mother. Women have even taken over Skid Row.

Life for the American man is like life with the governess in *The Turn of the Screw*; there are some good days, but sooner or later something awful happens and he's in the soup again.

The Iranian hostage crisis, coming as it did at the end of the decade of feminism, created an unparalleled crisis in American manhood. For the first time, a head of state cast open aspersions on the masculinity of an American president, thereby emasculating all American men. Pakistan's General Zia, an Alpha male if ever there was one, advised Jimmy Carter to "act like the president of a superpower," while an Asian diplomat at the United Nations sneered, "America is like your wife, always around for another beating."

Our pundits took up their scalpels, consulting, so it seemed, Roget's listings under *feminine* to describe the Carter personality. Robert Thompson called him "the Mona Lisa." George Will used *hysteria, shrillness*, and *frenzy*. William Safire produced *unrestrained restraint, self-flagellating, unprecedented weakness, acquiescing*, and *caving in*. Jack Anderson used *wavering, waffling, rhetorical tsk-tsks, pusillanimous, obsequious, hesitancy*, and *wishy-washy*. But the most frequently used word was *impotent*.

Joseph Kraft's prediction, "a disgust is building and Carter will pay," echoed Lamartine's reference to the "revolution of contempt" of 1848, when the French overthrew the Carter-like King Louis Philippe, who so abhorred symbols of power that he removed the fleurs-de-lis from the Palais Royal and referred to himself as the "Citizen King."

We got rid of the helpless Carter, but as things turned out it was just another turn of the screw. Far from ending, the masculinity crisis worsened during the Reagan years, whose most revealing visual metaphor was the crestfallen face of Eugene Hasenfus, the hunk with hurt feelings, emerging from the jungle looking like a macho poor soul.

From Edwin Meese's pouty mouth and wounded eyes

to Robert McFarlane's suicide attempt with pills instead of a gun, the stand-tall administration gave off a pervasive sense of emasculation. Sometimes it spilled over into effeminacy. The favorite political buzzword of the eighties, "mean-spirited," has a definite hiss to it and cannot be uttered without an accompanying sniff. The endless stream of retractions and clarifications that poured forth from the Reaganites recalled sorority house upheavals. Girlish double emphasis flew fast and furious as reporters grilled the stand-tall clarifier on what he *really* said, while he insisted that he *never* said such a thing and tried to explain what he *really* meant.

The feminization of poverty is just one aspect of a larger feminization of America. Pressure groups are increasingly pushing us toward government by nagging and cajolery; the slightest slip of the tongue by a politician brings forth shrill demands for apologies that brush perilously close to "If you don't take it back, I'll never speak to you again as long as I *live!*"

Politicians of both parties are in a race to prove that they have an acceptable supply of female traits. They boast incessantly about their "caring 'n' compassion"—the " 'n' factor" having been beatified in "women 'n' children," "blacks 'n' Hispanics," "education 'n' awareness." If their boasts are convincing, audiences will cheer them—not with whistles or clenched fists but by waving a pointed index finger in the air like a henpecker in full throttle.

Logic, long cherished by men as the premier male trait, came under fire during the Bork hearings, when female "feeling" became the order of the day. Bork was too "detached" and "objective" to be a judge, said his opponents; he must be seen as "seeming to care" if he wanted to be on the Supreme Court.

The feminization of America reached apogee in the political conventions of 1988 when the nominees for the most demanding job in the world boasted about how much time they spend with their families. That longstanding butt of male jokes and cartoons, the Family Man, was having a heyday. There were children all over the place, making speeches about Daddy, nominating Daddy, hugging Daddy, while the television cameras panned over the smoke-free room picking out mother-delegates with babes in arms. At the end, we got a ceremony that will surely produce a new word for American English: the "Familee," wherein the candidate rounds up every relative he can lay hands on and drags them up on the platform to play with balloons.

Watching the 1988 conventions and listening to the maudlin tributes to the Family Man, I recalled a very different tribute delivered more than sixty years ago. When Calvin Coolidge, Jr. was working on a farm during his summer vacation, another boy said to him, "If my father were president, I wouldn't work on a farm." Young Coolidge replied, "If my father were your father you would."

For once, I wished I were married to a presidential candidate so I could grab the microphone at the Familee and say: "The children are scared to death of him—all he has to do is *look* at them."

One of the worst problems the American man has to deal with is the American woman's love affair with reification.

To *reify* means to regard as material or concrete that which is not. It's a natural mental process that everyone indulges in from time to time. Longing for electricity on a primitive oil-lit chicken ranch in *The Egg and I*, Betty MacDonald came to think of kilowatts as peppercorns.

The vitamin has been reified. A chemical intangible originally defined as a unit of nutritive value, it was long ago reified into a pill. Now it *is* a pill; no one except a few precise scientists defines it as anything else. Once the vitamin became a pill, it became "real" according to the precepts of American Cartesianism: "I swallow it, therefore it is." The same thing has happened to the calorie, which That Cosmo Girl thinks of as a grinning demon with human capacities for sabotage and betrayal.

These examples of reification are harmless enough. The trouble starts when we get into deeper areas of human relationships.

When Freudianism crossed the ocean and made *ego* a household word, the male ego took shape in the American woman's mind as a large gaseous bubble ever in danger of deflation from a stray pin. Teeth and a digestive system were added when women's magazines started running articles about the "care and feeding" of it. Gradually the flesh became Word, so to speak, as the female subconscious turned men into their own egos. Men picked up the idea and ran with it, proudly staking their claim to abnegation by saying, in effect, *"Mon ego, c'est moi."*

The reification of marriage reveals the American woman in all her sexless vainglory. The wildly popular *Ladies Home Journal* column called "Can This Marriage Be Saved?" triggers instant visions of a passenger named Marriage singing "Nearer, My God, To Thee" on the deck of the *Titanic*.

In *From Housewife to Heretic*, former Mormon goodwife Sonia Johnson said that her husband left her because "he was tired of working on our marriage." It gets better. In an interview with Nancy Reagan, Eleanor Harris Howard asked, "How does one keep a marriage lastingly happy?" Mrs. Reagan replied, "Any marriage has to be worked on. It takes nourishing—you can't just let it lie there."

Think about that. The American woman's concept of marriage is a clearly etched picture of something uninflated on the floor. A sleeping bag without air, a beanbag without beans, a padded bra without pads. To work on it, you start pumping—what the magazines call "breathing life into your marriage." Do enough of this and the marriage becomes a kind of Banquo's ghost, a quasi-living entity that prevents the couple from ever being alone together until, as with the Johnsons, the reified marriage comes between them and they get a divorce.

In an argument with Plato, Antisthenes the Cynic defended nominalism by saying, "I see a horse, but I do not see horseness." American women see horseness everywhere.

American men have very few masculine stances left. If they want to show that they can *take it*, they can go without a coat on bitterly cold winter days, like Gary Hart shivering in the New Hampshire dawn; or Ronald Reagan shivering in Geneva while Gorbachev, who is used to much colder weather, bundled up in coat, scarf, and hat and regarded him with undisguised bemusement. "Where's your coat?" asked the translator. "Oh, I left it inside," the other translator replied manfully.

Alternatively, men can become terrorists and practice an updated version of the chivalric "women and children first" by releasing their female captives immediately—an extremely wise move for anyone wishing to practice terrorism in peace and quiet.

They can get convicted of first-degree murder and request execution for the purpose of dying bravely before witnesses. Gary Gilmore and Jesse Bishop both died bravely; Gilmore with stoicism and Bishop with jauntiness, calling for a bottle of booze and a woman for his final meal—classic male responses to danger and destruction designed to prove that Beau Geste is alive and well on Death Row.

And for men who want to flee Family Man America

and never come back, there is a guaranteed solution: homosexuality is the new French Foreign Legion.

One of the most striking examples of last-ditch masculinity that has cropped up lately is the way baseball has turned into football. Long the Jack-be-nimble game in which height and a big build are unimportant and can even be a drawback, baseball has found ways to stand tall. The team at bat and the team in the field are now called the "offense" and the "defense." Unnecessary roughness being almost impossible to manage in this most spread-out of games, pitchers have taken to hitting batters with the ball. Much of it has to be intentional; I never saw it happen when I was going to games during my first tomboyhood, but now, in my second, I see it dozens of times in a season.

And then there are the new uniforms. The chaste baggy flannels that served the important purpose of soaking up summer sweat have been replaced by skintight stretch pants to permit football-style crotch-and-ass flaunting, and the gridiron's glare-deflecting black cheekbone smudges are now sported on the diamond by men in visored caps who want to look ferocious.

Almost as pathetic was the grim head-'em-off-at-the-pass atmosphere surrounding Coca-Cola's decision to change its longstanding recipe. "Now we're willing to take risks," said company chairman Roberto C. Goizueta out of the side of his mouth. Company spokesman Carlton Curtis squared his jaw and added, "You're talking about having some guts—and doing something that few managements would have the guts to do." It's true that a great deal of money was at stake, but talking about courage and recipes in the same breath made these men sound idiotic.

These are the confused and wounded males that Shere Hite finds insufficiently sensitive and vulnerable. Don't try to disagree with her because she has statistics to back up her accusations. We're talking about research—and doing things that few researchers would have the guts to do:

1. Have you stopped hating men?
   ——yes ——no
2. How many men have you fantasized murdering?
   ——100 ——50–100 ——25–50
   ——less than 25
3. Check the word that best completes the sentence: "The worst thing about men is their im—"
   a. potence
   b. modesty
   c. placability
   d. pertinence
   e. perviousness
   f. petigo
4. Check the word that best completes the sentence: "My current lover/husband is un—"
   a. kind
   b. available
   c. concerned
   d. stable
   e. couth
   f. ctuous
5. Check the word that best completes the sentence: "Every man I meet is pre—"
   a. sumptuous
   b. tentious
   c. varicating
   d. occupied
   e. posterous
   f. ppy
6. Check the word that best completes the sentence: "All men are in—"
   a. ferior
   b. fernal
   c. ept
   d. ert

   e. ane
   f. grates
7. Which of the following historical figures makes you think of your current lover/husband?
   a. Ivan the Terrible
   b. Pippin the Short
   c. Peter the Hermit
   d. Louis the Pious
   e. William the Silent
   f. Ethelred the Unready
8. In which of the following great works of literature would you expect to find your current lover/husband?
   a. *The Idiot* by Fyodor Dostoyevsky
   b. *Polyeucte, Martyr* by Pierre Corneille
   c. "The Rape of the Lock" by Alexander Pope
   d. *Bleak House* by Charles Dickens
   e. *The Hairy Ape* by Eugene O'Neill
   f. *Dead Souls* by Nicolai Gogol
9. Which of the following musical works best expresses your experiences with men?
   a. The Unfinished Symphony
   b. The Trout Quintet
   c. "A Rambling Wreck From Georgia Tech"
   d. "The Picture That's Turned Toward the Wall"
   e. "Where Did Robinson Crusoe Go With Friday on Saturday Night?"
   f. "She's More to Be Pitied Than Censured"

   If Shere Hite were an unreconstructed Southerner, her mind would work like this: "I have nothing against men as long as they stay in their place. There're some nice men, I'm the first to admit it. Why, I used to play with a little man back when I was a young 'un. They're so cute when they're little—I tell you, there's nothing cuter than a little man. If only they'd stay little. . . . Now, I believe in being fair, but it we let up on them they'll take it as a sign of weakness and just go hogwild. I feel sorry for the nice men, I really do—and let me tell you, I'd rather live next door to nice men than trashy women—but you know what they say. Men might be nice all week, but when Saturday night comes around they turn into *guys*, and you know what they say—once you've been a guy on Saturday night you'll never want to be anything else."

I wish Shere Hite or some other feminist would explain to me what is so wonderful about "vulnerable" men. Too rich a diet of male vulnerability does things to women, and if you don't believe it, look at Rosalynn Carter's mean mouth. Better yet, reflect on Gen. George S. Patton's maxim, "Men who won't fight won't fuck."

It's time for American women to stop wailing "He never talks to me!" and let men be men, instead of fashioning dross out of gold and calling it "humanized." Men have always had their own brand of sensitivity, and the world thrilled to it long before Shere Hite was a cast in her daddy's eye.

One of the most sensitive men who ever lived was a foot soldier in the English army in 1431. No one knows his name. He must have been a roughneck and a drunkard, and a wife-and-child beater in the medieval manner. Probably he was a rapist, perhaps even a murderer. But he fashioned a cross for Joan of Arc out of wood from her pyre, and her last coherent words, "God bless you," were spoken to him.

Anyone who fears that letting men be men will endanger women and turn back the feminist clock should contemplate the words of Cervantes: "The woman who is resolved to be respected can make herself so even amidst an army of soldiers."

6 DOES YOUR CHILD TASTE SALTY?

The next earnest voice you hear will not be mine. I am sick of Helpism and its handmaidens, Education 'n' Awareness.

Bleating "I want to help people" used to be a temporary aberration of sophomore sociology majors, but today we have an entrenched Helpism industry. Helpists are everywhere, complete with toll-free telephone numbers composed of the letters H-E-L-P so we can call up and get more information on the afflictions that keep Cliff Robertson and Sally Struthers awake and tossing.

Helpists have a fiendish habit of running their public service announcements during shows that appeal to escapists. A three A.M. showing of *Wuthering Heights* stars Lawrence Olivier, Merle Oberon, and the Laird of Cystic Fibrosis Manor asking, "Does your child taste salty?" Many Helpist messages segue so seamlessly into the feature film that it's hard to tell one from the other, *e.g.*, a Vincent Price wax museum movie and the Narcolepsy Awareness minidrama about the girl who falls asleep at her mother's funeral while the church organ pumps out a dirge.

Many Helpists are simply funny, as earnest, half-baked people are always funny. Dickens had his philanthropic Mrs. Jellyby, who deprived her own children of milk so she could contribute to the African children's milk fund. America has Andie Blanton of Melbourne, Florida, who lost a python when it slithered into hiding somewhere in her car. According to the AP, she was taking it to school "as a classroom pet for her 10 *emotionally disabled* students, she said." [my italics]

Far more insidious is the Helpism that crawls out of the woodwork whenever a student commits suicide or dies in an accident.

> Immediately, a school crisis team goes into action. A representative at the student's school gets to work, collecting information on what happened. Then additional team members move in, breaking the news to teachers and students, setting up counseling sessions to help the school deal with the loss, the grief. Throughout the school, teachers and counselors will be on the lookout for students especially troubled by the news. Their focus—to prevent emotional problems and something known as "the cluster effect," a tendency of one teen suicide to be followed by several others. [the Fredericksburg, Virginia *Free Lance-Star*]

School suicide squads are the wave of the future according to King George County social worker Allen Mikszewski, who explains: "This sort of thing is just starting in Virginia, with Fairfax and Virginia Beach and a few other places the only other school systems developing programs. There's no one trained in it, and few authorities on the subject. We're breaking new ground."

If that sounds suspiciously eager, stand by for some unabashed drooling. The above-mentioned article goes on to say: "Teachers will be trained to look for trouble signs from students overcome with grief and depression. Still to be decided is whether all students would be automatically seen or addressed by the crisis team, or whether just particular groups or classes will get that attention."

Social worker Mikszewski has no intention of excusing anybody from crisis counseling: "If we don't see all of the students, there is always the risk that one shy, withdrawn student who won't ask for help is the one that we really need to see." Translated from Helpese, this means that any youngster with dignity and self-control will become a special target of the Clammy Ones.

Anyone who could read this article without getting a cold chill deserves to live in America. The school crisis team, with its counseling tables set up in the hall like a morbid version of Career Day, encourages kids to make a career out of falling apart. Inviting adolescents to emote is bound to be crowned with success. As girls do most of the emoting, the school crisis team perpetuates the stereotype of the unstable female. At the same time, it exerts a subtle pressure on boys to prove their "vulnerability" at an age when proof of vulnerability can leave males with permanent psychological scars.

A girl in my high school committed suicide when I was sixteen. The next day the student body was quieter than usual, but nobody broke down. Since the deceased had been in my homeroom, I was one of the group of girls officially designated to represent our class at the observances. Somewhere between the wake and the funeral, several Southern grandmothers got into the act with a dispute about some point of etiquette. I think it had to do with calling cards—it usually does—and by the time it was over (not settled, just over), we were all drained of every drop of emotion. We went to the funeral in a state of exhausted stoicism, completely wrung out and nerveless from coping with old ladies huffing "I never *heard* of such a thing in all my born days!"

What happened to us was precisely what is supposed to happen to people caught up in a sudden death: our emotions were dominated and redirected by the trivia of civilized behavior. As Mary McCarthy wrote in *The Group*: "You found that you got obsessed with these petty details. They were supposed to distract you from your grief. In fact, that was just what they did. You caught yourself forgetting the reason you were doing all this: because Kay had died. And the relief of finally arriving at a decision or having it taken out of your hands, as when Lakey got the dress, made you feel positively gay, till you remembered."

Since there can't possibly be anything pleasant about having several hundred hysterical teenagers on one's hands, it is time to wonder why these school crisis teams are doing everything in their power to encourage displays of inconsolable grief.

I daresay they do it out of love—specifically, love of money. Helpism of this sort is not without precedent. In her 1985 book, *The Weaker Vessel: Women in 17th-Century England*, Antonia Fraser tells us that in 1643, the financially desperate midwives of the realm petitioned the government to end the long French war and "return husbands to their wives, to bring them yearly under the delivering power of the midwife."

This obscure little footnote of history is disturbingly relevant vis-à-vis today's burgeoning supply of ostensibly compassionate counselors of drug addicts, unmarried mothers, battered wives, and abused children—all of whom would be out of work if the supply of drug addicts, unmarried mothers, battered wives, and abused children were to dry up.

* * *

My Sunday paper contained a curious insert, a whole section called "Support Groups" that turned out to be a directory of local conversational clearing houses for every conceivable form of trouble and strife known to human-kind. They included Life Management Seminar, Stress Management Workshop, Depression Resources, and Chronic Pain Outreach, to name just a few.

The proliferation of support groups suggests to me that too many Americans are growing up in homes that do not contain a grandmother. A home without a grandmother is like an egg without salt, and Helpists know it. They have jumped into the void left by the disappearance of morbid old ladies from the bosom of the American family. The emotionally satisfying discussions that take place in Chronic Pain Outreach and Depression Resources are simply updated versions of the grandmotherly practice of hanging crepe. We could eliminate much of the isolation that support groups exist to fill and save the "traditional family" that everybody is so worried about if more couples took their aging parents to live with them.

Having a grandmother in residence makes books and articles on "How to Help Your Child Cope With Death" totally unnecessary. We tend to assume that old people fear death, but somehow I doubt it. . . .

"Oh, good, the paper's come! Let's see who died." Expertly inserting her thumb into the obits section, Granny began to read. "I knew it! Look at the story the family's giving out. 'Sudden stroke,' indeed! I heard that she was really murdered in the beauty parlor. They say the dye got in her ear and went all through her system until it reached her heart and killed her. That's what you get for dyeing your hair. . . . Oh, here's poor Mr. Jordan. You know he choked to death at the table? Aunt Cora's cousin's niece died that way. They say her mother reached down her throat to pull the bone out and pulled all her insides out with it. She just kept pulling and pulling, and they just kept coming and coming, until it was all there on the table and the undertaker hardly had any work to do. He only charged them half-price."

To make sure I learned the etiquette of grieving, Granny took me with her to the many funerals she attended. *O Death, where is thy sting?* Search me. I grew up looking at so many corpses that I still feel a faint touch of surprise whenever I see people move.

One of the reasons today's children are such sheeplike conformists who won't make a move without checking their peer pressure is that they are never exposed to old people in the fullness of their carte blanche. In his essay "On Liberty," John Stuart Mill wrote: "Eccentricity has always abounded when and where strength of character has abounded; and the amount of eccentricity in a society has generally been proportional to the amount of genius, mental vigor, and moral courage which it contained."

Helpists hate eccentrics because people who march to a different drummer never follow the pied pipers of Education 'n' Awareness. Television's dullest public service announcement is the osteoporosis pitch that shows a young woman on a train regarding with mixed pity and dread a bent-over old lady struggling painfully into her seat. Neither woman seems to have any personality whatsoever; although they sit opposite each other for the duration of the trip, they never even say hello. All the talking is done by the earnest voice-over; the women sit there in total silence with Calcium Awareness looming between them like a stone wall.

If Granny were cast as the old lady, the pitch would go like this:

"My, what a nice straight back you have, honey. I had a straight back when I was your age; I could walk down the steps with a book on my head. Now I'm so bent over I find six dimes every day. They say a dowager's hump will make you rich! Old bones, that's what it is, old bones. The Change does it, you know—after you stop coming unwell, you lose all your marrow. It's got to come to all of us someday. My mother's sister-in-law's cousin knew a poor soul who got so bent-over that one day she just went *pop!* and broke right in half. They had to put her back together again in the coffin, but they didn't lay her out right and it showed."

I maintain that this is more interesting than droning milligram counts. Granny's old wives' tale might or might not raise the young woman's Calcium Awareness, but it would certainly raise her hair, and give her a train ride to dine out on for years to come. Take my word for it: If a child grows up tooling around with a grandmother who buttonholes strangers and strikes up conversations that leave them bug-eyed with wonderment, he will never wind up in Crack Outreach because he feared being "different" from his strung-out peer group.

Much of today's Helpism is nothing but old-fashioned "interference." American couples have gone to such lengths to avoid the interference of in-laws that they have to pay marriage counselors to interfere between them. Resident grandmothers do it for free. My parents were so mismatched that the only thing they had in common was me, but they coexisted successfully because Granny's imposing presence "interfered" with the kind of intimate privacy that neither of them was emotionally equipped to handle. When she died and they were alone together at last, all hell broke loose.

Let's face it. There aren't many divinely happy marriages to interfere with, but there are plenty that could use a good buffer state. Plenty could use a built-in babysitter, too. The Day Care Hot Line would cool down fast if today's working mothers were as carefree as mine was. The idea is afoot nowadays that all grandmothers are straining at the bit the "live their own lives." They are told that they really ought to want to cruise the South Pacific, live alone in a high-rise apartment, and have affairs. What most of them really want is their grandchildren.

Grandmothers don't spoil children; tired parents do. The purpose of discipline is self-discipline, and its best source is the full-time, hovering presence of a grandmother. Granny set out to raise me to be a perfect Southern lady, but she could not have done a better job of raising a writer. Her constant nagging admonitions to "sit up straight . . . keep still . . . finish what you start" are what enable me to sit at the word processor for ten or twelve hours at a stretch. That's what I call *help*.

At fifty-two I have no need for the ministrations of the Menopause Seminar because I am not afraid of getting old. Living with Granny taught me that aging does not make women powerless objects of pity but colorful and entertaining individuals, and on occasion, fire-breathing dragons that wise people don't cross.

A real family consists of three generations. We could screw the Helpists out of existence if we stopped worrying about interference and being a burden on each other and regrouped under one roof.

Thanks to my early conditioning, old people are the only people whose company I enjoy and seek out. To the best of my memory and knowledge, I never met an old person I didn't like, or who didn't like me. We're a felicitous combination, so you can imagine how I feel when I receive, on the first of every month, a piece of mail containing a pseudo-compassionate Helpist ploy aimed at them.

Those foremost practitioners of Thugee, public utility companies, have moved in on Christian charity. Listen to Virginia Electric Power's version of the temporal act of mercy:

Help us help someone you love. If you know an elderly or infirm Vepco customer who could benefit from our Third Party Notice program, please tell us.

Elderly or infirm customers sometimes forget to pay their electric bills or, because of their illnesses, are unable to handle their financial affairs. To help protect these customers from losing their electric service because of past-due bills, Vepco offers the *Third Party Notice* program. We mail a copy of the disconnect notice to a third party—relative, clergyman, social agency, close friend or anyone designated by the customer. This extra notice does not mean the third party must pay the bill. It merely informs the party of the past-due bill so that he or she can take steps to assure continued service.

Behold the Helpists in all their power-mad glory—they want us to help them hound old people.

The prophet of America's religion of Helpism was Dale Carnegie, whose landmark 1937 book, *How to Win Friends and Influence People*, was the opening wedge in the promotion of personality over character. Today's Helpists have gone much further. By their insidious pandering to hypochondria and fear of death, they have destroyed the old virtues and replaced them with mere good habits. Honor, duty, and steadfastness are now called diet, exercise, and non-smoking.

Helpism's modus operandi is very simple: find something that reminds Americans of death and go to the mat with it. One such subject is sleep.

It's said that Michael Dukakis gets only four or five hours of sleep a night. I believe it: he looks as if somebody started to embalm him and then stopped. Between success-driven maxims like "The early bird gets the worm" and the old puritanical fear of beds in general, we are the groggiest people in history. The latest victims of our national wakefulness are working mothers who do their housework at three A.M. Women used to be able to go back to bed after their husbands left for work, or take a nap along with the baby, but now they're half-dead along with everybody else.

About the only way left to shock people nowadays is to say, as I make a point of saying whenever I get a chance, that you *need* and *get* nine or ten hours of sleep every night. At least one member of your audience will start babbling about some article called "Do You Sleep Too Much?" (what other country would publish such a thing?), and before you know it, they're all babbling about "sleep as escape from problems" and telling you to "seek help."

Nothing arouses American conflicts like the subject of sleep. Sleep is intimately connected with things we refuse to talk about, as well as the things we talk about constantly. Our contradictory attitudes toward sleep are the litmus paper for all of our contradictions as a people. There is nothing about sleep that doesn't remind us of something else about sleep that triggers anxiety. Sleep is thus a gold mine for Helpists. Consider the number of How To/Are You/Do You books that a resourceful Helpist could extract from the following:

"I don't need much sleep." The Tom Edison complex.

"Napping in the daytime makes you feel worse." The Gringo complex.

"Don't those people ever sleep?" The Wasp complex.

"Secretary of State Darius McTavish went forty-eight hours without sleep." The Awesome Responsibilities complex.

"Despite having gone without sleep for forty-eight

hours, McTavish appeared rested and relaxed." The Omnipotence complex.

"McTavish dozed for an hour on the plane." The Common Touch complex.

"Help someone you love fall asleep." The Supportiveness complex.

"Makes you drowsy so you can fall asleep." The Rugged Individualist complex.

"I don't have time to sleep." The Workaholic complex.

"Don't lose any sleep over it." The Nine-to-Five complex.

"We didn't get any sleep last night!" That Cosmo Girl complex.

"If the world blew up while you were asleep, you'd want David Truehart of *Turn Over, America* to tell you about it." The Unthreatening Personality complex.

"Sleep on it." The Decisive complex.

"It kept me awake." The Concerned complex.

"I slept like a log." The Clear Conscience complex.

"I slept through it." The Anti-Intellectual complex.

"Shall we wake the president?" The Leader complex.

"There was no need to wake the president." The Team-Player complex.

"Secretary of State Darius McTavish died in his sleep last night." The Quick 'n' Easy complex.

Helpism's first cousin is self-helpism. Speaking on the subject of giving advice, Catherine the Great said: "A strong mind is not suited for advising a weak one, for it is incapable of following the thoughts of the latter."

Today's self-help authors will never have to worry about that. They make Ann Landers sound like Descartes.

Honorable Intentions: The Manners of Courtship in the '80s by Cheryl Merser contains a chapter called "The Sleep-Over Date" in which she assures men: "You will find that your new lover's bathroom is a source of wonder and surprise. This, you'll think, is the toothbrush she brushes her teeth with morning and night, and here are her cotton balls."

All self-help authors are obsessed with checklists, but Merser tops them all when she advises manufacturers of birth control products to include in their packages a checklist that reads: "Now that you have your Pills, have you thought of the following? Fresh coffee, towels, sheets, croissants, flowers? Is your date planned with a free morning tomorrow? Did you buy candles, firewood? If you bought firewood, do you have a fireplace?"

A fire without a fireplace would certainly be a night to remember, but unconscious humor is a fixture of this genre. In *How to Find a Husband in 30 Days*, Wendy Stehling couches her advice in a series of unforgettable tips:

"TIP: When you are going to meet men, get dressed."

"TIP: THE RACE TRACK: During the week—anytime—stand at the paddock and ask if the bay horse is lame in the left foreleg."

Worse than the unconscious humor are the bold attempts at wit. Merser describes a cheapskate as "Penny, a member of the Pincher family," while Gail Kessler's *How to Marry a Good Man* recommends icebreakers like "How about coming over for a cup of hemlock?"

At some point in every sexual self-help book we encounter a passage that lends credence to Santayana's observation, "A life of pleasure requires an aristocratic setting to make it interesting or really conceivable." With Wendy Stehling, it's the reassurance that "Men aren't looking for beauty and money, they aren't even looking for a high IQ." But that Merser should feel it necessary to tell her readers never to eat peanut butter straight from the jar with their fingers while their lovers are watching suggests that the English duchess who reputedly said "Sex is too good for the common people" was right.

Self-help books are making life downright unsafe. Women desperate to catch a man practice all the ploys recommended by these authors. Bump into him, trip over him, knock him down, spill something on him, scald him, but *meet him*. That little fender-bender calculated to make him get out of his car and exchange phone numbers could turn into a twelve-car pile-up.

Worse, self-help books are bad for dogs. Rare is the advice giver who does not recommend using dogs as ice-breakers. Walking one's dog in order to meet a man who is walking his dog requires a dog, whether one wants a dog or not, whether one likes dogs or not. As a result, the country is full of unhappy, unwanted, neglected dogs. I don't care what people do to each other but I love dogs. Anyone seen reading a self-help book should be reported to the Humane Society at once.

Many readers of self-help books are the kind of people who used to enter nunneries and monasteries in medieval times: passive, ethereal, low-sexed individuals unable to cope with the vicissitudes of ordinary living. Despite its brutalities and superstititions, the Middle Ages was an essentially well-adjusted era because it did not make its misfits worse by urging them to social and sexual triumphs beyond their capacities. That many Americans yearn for such a world was made manifest by the commune movement, which was less a political statement than a subconscious attempt by tender souls to revive the cloister.

Self-helpism reaches its zenith in Jimmy and Rosalynn Carter's guide to retirement, *Everything to Gain: Making the Most of the Rest of Your Life*.

Devout Christians are not supposed to fear death, but that is precisely the dark thread running through this chapbook of altruisitic delights, which kicks off with: "Every day the average life expectancy of Americans increases by seven hours—two days each week, twenty-five years in this century."

A little later the point is made again: "It was startling to find that a person can lose as many as a dozen years of potential life by adhering to certain habits. We had never realized how much control we actually have over how long we might live."

And again: ". . . a fifty-year-old man or woman today who keeps risk factors low can expect to live eleven years longer than contemporaries who don't follow such approaches. Eleven years!"

Given this eleven-year itch, it comes as no surprise to learn that the Carter Center at Emory University has a computer that can tell people how long they can expect to live. "It should be helpful and possibly even fun," says Jimmy, "for participants to see just what they can do to extend their life spans."

Future historians will say that nothing so became the Carter life span as the extending of it. Their fitness program, described with the passion for detail that Jimmy brought to White House tennis court schedules, now fills their days. They jog, exercise to Jane Fonda tapes, watch their diets, buckle their seat belts, and fret. "The chances of being fatally injured in an automobile accident can be cut in half by the use of seat belts. Cut in half!" Jimmy cries out in the wilderness. In calmer moments, he is still the master of the sanctimonious sniff. Boasting quietly that he has never smoked, he adds: "Unfortunately, my mother, my two sisters, and my brother all followed my father's example and became heavy smokers. The two who survive have broken the habit but the others died of cancer."

The Carters describe how they joined Habitat for Humanity and built houses for the poor. The experience was so satisfying that they looked around for other Helpist groups to join and listed their findings in the back of their book. It's better to be a Pink Lady than to drink one, but if nursing isn't your bag, "Special Olympics groups need

74

many 'huggers' to encourage retarded athletes, and some hospital nurseries use volunteer huggers to stimulate low-birth-weight babies."

Altruism like this can't be contained in one country, so the Carters went people-to-peopling in the Third World. This part of the book is more fun than a brother-in-law's vacation slide lecture: "We visited homes and schools for children of parents suffering from leprosy." That mission of mercy done, they climbed a mountain in Nepal, where Bubba spotted a Gompa (that's a Buddhist monastery, not the man-eating tiger I was hoping for).

Like Dickens's Mrs. Jellyby, the Carters have forgotten that charity begins at home. If they're so hot to help somebody they need look no further than their daughter Amy. The pictures taken of her at her anti-nuke protest trial in Massachusetts leave no doubt that she needs a great deal more than the "supportiveness" her sap of a father bestowed on her misadventures.

It was obvious that health, mental or physical, is not her long suit. The pasty skin, the blank eyes, the toneless voice, the stringy, greasy, half-black, half-blond hair, the just-plain-dirty look of her, all suggest not a return to hippie chic but the collapse of fastidiousness that presages a nervous breakdown.

Amy Carter is well on the way to becoming that favorite American sickie known as a "poor little rich girl." During the Depression thirties, we devoured endless news stories about unhappy Barbara Hutton, the Woolworth heiress; unhappy Doris Duke, the tobacco heiress; unhappy Gloria Vanderbilt, the heiress heiress; and unhappy Brenda Frazier, the debutante who came out in 1938 and spent the rest of her life coming apart.

Since then, inherited money has given way to fame as the source of fashionable misery, and beauty has given way to "correct" politics as the source of fame, so a new kind of poor little rich girl is in order.

75

For a while it looked as if Jane Fonda would succeed to the crown, but she eliminated herself by developing staying power—staying out of the news, staying out of jail, staying married—so she's a goner. Amy Carter is a comer, and it promises to be a long haul. I won't live to see all of it, thank God, but I remember enough about her forerunners of the thirties to make some educated guesses about the milestones:

She will acquire a Latin lover who will beat her up in the bar of the Essex House.

She will have an affair with an updated version of Howard Hughes, who at this point seems to be Ted Turner.

She will marry an impotent intellectual and testify at the annulment hearing about the perverted things he did to her feet.

She will be photographed at the precise moment when her second husband, a famous athlete, throws champagne in her face.

She will convert to Catholicism, Orthodox Judaism, and Christian Science.

She will be found wandering around downtown Istanbul in a state of amnesia.

She will balloon up to two hundred pounds and starve herself down to ninety pounds with diet pills.

She will be arrested for shoplifting.

She will drop out of sight for several years and turn up as the wife of a lumberjack in Forks, Washington.

She will make a comeback and host her own talk show.

She will announce on camera that she is entering the Betty Ford Clinic.

She will emerge from the Betty Ford Clinic to headlines announcing the "New Amy" and marry the famous movie actor from her therapy group.

She will find him in bed with a man and slit her wrists.

She will say "At last I've found happiness" when she marries the Long Island vet.

She will be photographed throwing herself into the lumberjack's grave and commune with his spirit in the *National Enquirer*.

She will sue the plastic surgeon for the bad face-lift.

He will write *Ironing Out the Wrinkles: How to Survive Professional Lawsuits*.

She will get another face-lift and take up with a beach boy young enough to be her grandson.

She will write *Help Yourself to Youth*.

The beach boy will write *Once in Love With Amy: How to Make Love to an Older Woman*.

His book will be withdrawn by the publisher the day after Amy is rushed to the hospital with a ruptured vagina.

Lear's magazine will run "Ten Lubrication Aids for the Woman Who Wasn't Born Yesterday."

It will be expanded into a book called *The Problem With a Name: The Sahara Mystique*.

Amy will pass to her reward and her executor will write *Putting Your Affairs in Order: How to Prepare for Sudden Death*.

7

NICE GUYISM

I was shopping for groceries at Gulpmart, the Friendly Store, when a woman slithered up to me at the frozen food bin and whispered, "I love you. Pass it on."

She explained that she had been inspired by Hands Across America, and had decided to launch a verbal version of same.

"When you say it to children, kiss them," she advised.

The thought of actually kissing America's gross national product upset me so much that I made a mistake in the checkout line. Thinking to get even change for my $44.61 purchase, I gave the clerk a fifty-dollar bill and what I thought was a penny but which was in fact a dime.

"Trade you this for a penny!" she cried gaily.

She gave me a big American smile involving both rows of teeth. It isn't a smile, it's a rictus; the mouth simply drops open like a crocodile's. The banks of the Wabash have turned into the banks of the Amazon. Farrah Fawcett started it and now it has spread across America, along with hands and kisses and God knows what else. No normal jaw can manage it; I am convinced that these people have an operation to remove a piece of bone from each side.

I didn't take in what the clerk said. I was staring at her mouth, wondering if I could find a stick to prop it open before she got me.

"Trade you this dime for a penny?" she repeated, smiling harder.

Finally I realized that this was her friendly way of telling me I had made a mistake. As I fished out a penny I remembered that she was the same clerk who always said "What can I do you for?" instead of "What can I do for you?" because inverted wording is warmer—like bad grammar. The soft round sound of *loaned* is friendlier than the harshly linear but correct *lent*.

I went home, mixed a martini, and turned on the television. Three commercials in a row assured me that Eastern Air Lines, Allied Van Lines, and Ex-Lax—movers and shakers all—were my friends. Moreover, Ex-Lax was my *family* friend because it's gentle.

The phrase "gentle laxative" is oxymoronic to the sane mind. The confidence and security of a people can be measured by their attitude toward laxatives. At the high noon of the British sun, soldiers in far-flung outposts of the Empire doctored themselves with "a spoonful o' gunpowder in a cuppa 'ot tea." Purveyors and users of harsh laxatives were not afraid of being thought mean and unfriendly just because their laxatives were. But in America, the need to be nice is so consuming that nobody would dare take a laxative that makes you run up the stairs two at a time, pushing others aside and yelling "Get out of the way!" In no other country could Cascara, Syrup of Pepsin, and Citrate of Magnesia cause hurt *feelings*, but they could in America, so we have invented the gentle laxative to help us practice Nice Guyism of the bowels.

Sipping my martini, I watched a community service show. The guest, a psychologist engaged in discovering new minority groups, recommended that midgets be called "persons of reduced stature."

Next, some public service announcements. A lumber company claiming to be a friend of forests presented a celestial chorus singing "Thank a Tree." A woman in a grocery store stood beside a sign reading "Please Don't Squeeze the Tomatoes" and squeezed a tomato; the camera shifted to the seething grocer as the whispery voice-over said, "An ounce of love is worth a pound of anger."

Finally the news. Dan Rather, obediently sweltering in a V-neck sweater so he would be "perceived as warm," recited the ballad of Stephen Brill, New York City plant eater, who had been arrested the previous week for picking edible plants in Central Park. This unfriendly action drew so many citizen complaints that Fun City relented and gave Brill a job taking other herbiphiles on guided tours of edible plants at a salary of fifteen dollars an hour, compliments of New York taxpayers.

The Nice Guyism in the Brill episode is nothing compared with a 1980 story—one of my most cherished newspaper clippings—about a lad of seventeen who tried to hijack a plane at Seattle-Tacoma airport. After he was captured, a reporter interviewed the flight attendant, who said: "He was very cooperative, he's been almost a model hijacker."

In the spring of 1987 the United Methodist Church announced that it was placing a warning label in their hymnal beside the last stanza of "There Is a Fountain Filled With Blood" because it might offend the handicapped. In the spring of 1988 we had the radio listeners who sent in $240,000 to Dallas disc jockey Ron Chapman simply because he asked them to. He didn't shill anything, didn't promise anything; he just asked people to send in twenty dollars and they did.

Like medievalists keeping track of good and evil spirits, we divide people into "threatening" and "nonthreatening," the foremost example of the latter being that careful knee-crosser, David Hartman. Our favorite stances run the gamut from the characterless "nonjudgmental" to the meaningless "we're all human." Our friendly banks are robbed constantly because we reject the notion that an ounce of fear is worth a pound of love; all you have to do to get past a security guard is be human: the password is "Hi." Despite twenty years of feminism, women still get into trouble with strange men because they would rather be dead than aloof. Lest a bad mood be interpreted as a sign of sexual frustration, legions of singles (including the strange men) adopt an air of relentless cheer to prove they're getting it regularly.

Old people are so afraid of fitting the crotchety stereotype of age that they are suckers for bunco schemes that would fail in any other country. Doctors formerly in general practice are now in "family practice" because it sounds warmer. A few years ago, the Los Angeles police chief urged his officers to adopt a "warm and cuddly approach" to civilians to improve community relations. Not long after, Secretary of the Interior James Watt defended himself against charges of "insensitivity" by holding a press conference in which he announced, "I'm really warm and cuddly."

If you don't believe we're warm and cuddly, ask Canada. When she rescued six of our Iranian embassy hostages, our galumphing appreciation left Canadians reeling in shock. Later, when Algeria negotiated the release of the rest, we tried to snuggle up to her. Anyone who is nice to us is marked for death-by-slurp.

We are so dependent on the Nice Guyism of strangers that the first question American tourists ask about foreign countries, even before the exchange rate, is "Are the people friendly?" Leading the No list is that cradle of premenstrual tension, France, from whose shores Americans regularly return pale and trembling and lashing themselves with the masochistic question "What did I do wrong?" The simple truth—that the French are Friday farts at a Saturday market—never gets voiced. It's too unfriendly.

Nice Guyism produces a strange form of treason in the American heart. In our desperation to believe that we are not hated personally, we grasp at the political straw of anti-Americanism and blame French nastiness on American foreign policy. It works like a batty charm. Soothed by the belief that foreigners still like "us" regardless of what they may think of the the U.S., we relax and grow secure whenever terrorists and foamy revolutionaries say "It's the American government we hate, not the American people."

During the 1980 presidential campaign, Joseph Kraft wrote: "The emergence of President Carter and Ronald Reagan as the nearly certain nominees of their parties expresses not a failure of the system, but a true translation of how much the majority prefers nice men to effective measures."

We want a president who is as much like an American tourist as possible. Someone with the same goofy grin, the same innocent intentions, the same naive trust; a president with no conception of foreign policy and no discernible connection to the U.S. government, whose Nice Guyism will narrow the gap between the U.S. and us until nobody can tell the difference.

That the Ayatollah Khomeini did not fall for this panacea but lumped the American government, the American people, Hollywood movies, miniskirts, and *Playboy* under the same mantle of "Great Satan" traumatized us more than the coming Russian invasion is likely to do. After all, the Russians will have sense enough to teach their occupation troops how to say "Hi, I'm Ivan," which will make everything all right.

* * *

Why are Americans the Newfoundland puppies of the New World?

Our obsession with friendliness began when the first settlers wondered "Are the natives friendly?" and shortly found themselves looking at stoic Indian faces. The natives were friendly, at least at first, but they didn't *look* it. Unsmiling faces have struck terror in the American heart ever since.

Next we acquired the melting pot. There are so many different kinds of people in America, with so many different boiling points, that we don't know how to fight with each other. The set piece that shapes and contains quarrels in homogeneous countries does not exist here. The Frenchman is an expert on the precise gradations of *espèce de* and the Italian knows exactly when to introduce the subject of his mother's grave, but no American can be sure how or when another American will react, so we zap each other with friendliness to neutralize potentially dangerous situations.

The aloof warmth that makes life so pleasant in socially confident countries is not available to us, so we are forced to leap feet-first into cloying intimacy whether we like it or not. The tender formality of "*gnädige Frau*" makes old ladies easy to respect, and stiff Englishmen long ago learned to express intrasex affection with "my dear Smith," but Americans have nothing to call each other by except first names. There is no way to get a stranger's attention without sounding servile (ma'am, sir) and so, committed as we are to equality at any price, we insult him. Ironically, our Smile Button egalitarians have yet to grasp the fact that indiscriminate friendliness is a democratized version of the obsequiousness practiced by the lower classes in hierarchical societies throughout history.

Friendliness is a matter of life and death to people who live by the maxim, "The country is full of nuts." The chance victim and the innocent bystander have replaced the plucky newsboy and the whore with the heart of gold as the protagonists of American folklore. We have no idea "who's out there," so smile your way to safety. If you are cool to someone, he might tell the FBI lies about you, or send an anonymous letter to the IRS, or report you for child abuse, or haul off and shoot you—all because he doesn't like your face, so give everybody the Nice Guy treatment. Bridges of understanding are good but walls of friendliness are better.

Compulsive hugging is an excess whose time has come, but sensitivity workshops should not take all the credit for it. Much of it is simply an offshoot of America's transition from a Wasp to an ethnic culture. We have taken up studied emotionalism in the belief that everything will be all right if only we shed our bad old Anglo-Saxon ways. But there's a catch. Sang-froid is an indispensable quality to have when trying to obey the commercial that says "Never let them see you sweat."

Which way do we want it? Anglo-Saxon cool or Latin heat? We don't know; stripped of our old national persona yet lacking a fully developed new one, we're like analysands whose doctor has died suddenly in the middle of the analysis, or Marine Corps recruits halfway through boot camp, or recently molted crabs.

Fortunately, several commercials permit us to experiment with the national character. There's nothing like a thirty-second New You. If "Never let them see you sweat" is Wasp, the consumer protection ad "Don't take being taken" is ethnic, a leftover portion of the old greenhorn complex that emerged when immigrants just off the boat fell for the scam of buying the Brooklyn Bridge.

Our confusion over what to do about emotion may account for the many statements that are made and then immediately withdrawn, like Edwin Meese's hunger count. "There aren't any hungry people in America" (cold Wasp) followed by "There are hungry people in America" (warm ethnic) produced a hot-and-cold running Meese who typified his fellow countrymen.

A situation that requires the ultimate in Nice Guyism is one that I've had to endure on a regular basis.

Told that her latest London performance was a tour de force, Mrs. Patrick Campbell replied, "Then why am I forced to tour?" The purpose of a book tour, in the stunning logic of publishers, is "to reach the people who don't read books." I've reached them. They are the truffle hounds in America's hunt for threatening personalities, the same insecure pests who bawl "Whatcha lookin' so sad about?" or "Smile! It can't be that bad!" every time they see a pensive soul gazing into space. When not bothering strangers in airports, they hang around television stations, where they either host studio audience shows or serve as members of the audience.

On my early tours I was able to masquerade as warm and friendly provided my television spot lasted no longer than five minutes, but the last time out a kind of madness came over me and my mask began to slip.

"Why do you wear your hair like that?" asked a Birmingham interviewer, warily eyeing my skinned-back chignon.

"It gets me out of jury duty," I said. "The defense takes one look at me and says 'Challenge.' "

On another show a few days later, we were discussing the girlish games played at Southern bridal showers when suddenly the hostess interrupted with a reminiscence.

"The engagement ring my husband gave me was such a teeny-tiny, little ole stone that everybody thought it was a wedding ring and asked me if I'd eloped. I mean, it was the *littlest* stone I ever did see!"

"It must have been a recondite," I said.

Nobody got it, but they all knew that something had happened. Silence. Dropped-pin time. Dead air. Waves of hostility. The audience turned into Madame Defarge and I was the last of the Evremondes.

The most threatening image a touring writer can present is one of seriousness and depth. I was too tired to make this mistake but I can just imagine the smile-button assault it would trigger.

"Well, Ed, you've been pretty hard on the barbarians, but don't you think that extending the frontiers of the Empire gave the Romans a chance to meet new people?"

"Oswald, you can't mean all those things you said about the West. Don't you really think it's God's country?"

"Tom, what's it like to go year after year without talking? We want to hear all about your vow of silence. Tell us about life in a Trappist monastery and then we'll take some calls from our listeners. We've got some great listeners, Tom."

If you think the hosts are friendly, wait till you meet the escorts. Publishers are so busy being thoughtful that they never stop and think. Hiring a local resident to drive a touring author around to television and radio stations is an excellent idea because all call letters sound alike after a while. What publishers fail to consider is the kind of person the escort is likely to be.

Those who choose to work in a hospitality or official-greeter capacity do so because they "love people," which means they talk the hind legs off a mule. Thus, in addition to the four scheduled interviews you have that day, you also have a fifth, unscheduled, running interview with the escort, who asks the same questions asked by the friendly hosts at WXXI, WIXX, WXIX, and WIIX.

"Where do you get your ideas?"

"Do you write every day or just when you're inspired?"

"Do you use a typewriter or do you write by hand?"

Escorts wouldn't dream of sitting in the car and reading while the writer is performing in the studio. So you won't get lonely, they go in the Green Room with you and chat you up while you're waiting to go on.

"Just how do you go about getting an agent?"

"How does the copyright law work?"

"People have always told me I should write. 'If you could write the way you talk, you'd have a bestseller,' they always say."

Do you ever write poetry? I love poetry. 'When lilacs last in the door yard bloomed. . . .' "

"I love a good mystery. Have you ever thought of trying your hand at murder?"

"Yes."

Does it end now? It might not if it's a radio interview. When the gregarious host saw the escort sitting there with me, he invited her into the sound booth to sit in on the show, because a stranger is a friend you haven't met yet.

That was the show on which I said, "Sex is rough on loners; you have to have somebody else around."

No citizenry can practice Nice Guyism without some respite. Resisting car pools is an excellent way to be American and unfriendly at the same time; nobody will criticize you for loving your wheels. Other cracks in the Smile Button include the Tylenol poisoning, the Los Angeles freeway shoot-outs, the highly successful "People Hate Drunk Drivers" campaign, and of course, the knock-down, drag-out vituperation aimed at smokers.

But that's not all. When in the course of human events

it becomes necessary for a people to dissolve the treacly bands of molasses-across-America that connect them one to the other, they can always get off on a coffee commercial.

"Fill it to the rim with Brim" is the most violent expression of anal sadism this side of Krafft-Ebing.

8

DEMOCRAZY

At the Japanese war trials of 1946, the defunct empire's former propaganda minister, Shumei Okawa, inadvertently made a good pun. Leaping to his feet in fury, he screamed in his uncertain English: "I hate United States! It is democrazy!"

We get democrazier by the minute. The only things we discriminate against are smokers and bad hugs. Our blood is so rich with equality that we have come to hate uniqueness of any kind, no matter how noble. By having a Tomb of the Unknowns, we really don't have an Unknown Soldier—more than one destroys the concept.

We even hate the unique hatred. If, for example, someone hates gays, we suspect him of also hating blacks, Jews, Hispanics, Orientals, and Indians—and get mad if he doesn't.

Chi-chi liberals mourned the death of the Orient Express in a reverent "60 Minutes" segment, yet it is egalitarianism that has destroyed the kind of world that justifies luxury trains: Princess Dragomiroff needs Drawing Room A, and Drawing Room A needs Princess Dragomiroff.

It was only to be expected that the Nobel Prize Sperm Bank should have triggered such Lear-like rage. Particularly upset was Mary McGrory, who suggested that breeding reliable home repairmen would benefit society more. Her reason? "Workmen do not hear unless you scream at them, like police dogs who only respond to a certain high, piercing whistle. It is only when a certain level of frustration has been reached that he is able to judge the sincerity of the consumer and the persistence of his notion that the work may be done. He may oblige if he is persuaded that apoplexy or a lawsuit is not far away."

She begs the question. The attitudes to which she objects have resulted from our enshrinement of equality: if everybody is as good as everybody else, why should a plumber be respectful of a syndicated columnist? Especially when she momentarily forgets her "correct" politics and likens manual workers to dogs.

We go to pieces in the face of bigoted germs. America is the home of the Democratic Crud. Every article on every ailment always contains The Sentence: "Hepatitis [mononucleosis, herpes, shingles, kidney stones, the clap] strikes Americans of all socio-economic groups and educational levels without regard to race, national origin, or sex." If we could turn sickle-cell anemia and Tay-Sachs disease over to the Justice Department we would do so.

The year before AIDS was discovered the airwaves were full of voices thick with concern saying things like "Lung cancer is an equal opportunity disease." They launched into a history of cigarette smoking, pointing out that when it was considered unladylike, most women did not indulge and therefore did not get lung cancer, which led people to think it was a man's disease from which women were naturally immune. "But now," the Earnest One continued happily, "women are catching up."

The hysterical insistence that AIDS is "everybody's disease" finds us faced with the task of promoting safe sex without using elitist words like *choosy*. The current "tasteful" condom commercials will have to come down in the world so that we can get across the message that people who use condoms are no better than anybody else. This can be done if we show a motherly amazon pummeling the things and bellowing "They don't say Trojans till *I* say they say Trojans!" and a teenager saying "They're *my* parents, I tell you, and they're acting strange. Hmmm . . . whose is this?"

America can democratize anything. Imagine for a moment that we revived the "natural aristocrat" theory held by John Adams and other Founding Fathers. Somebody would go on "Nightline" and say "Everybody's gotta right to be a natural aristocrat," and then it would start: the Natural Aristocrat Task Force, the Natural Aristocrat Resources Center, the Natural Aristocrat Hot Line, the Natural Aristocrat Crisis Team, Natural Aristocrat Crash Programs, Natural Aristocrat Counseling, Natural Aristocrat Awareness, Natural Aristocrat Advocacy, Natural Aristocrat Month, and a bestseller entitled *How to Help Your Child Be a Natural Aristocrat.*

Our successful democratization of the middle class shows up in the construction worker's reply to the demographics pollster who asks him to rate himself on the social scale: "Aw, sorta middle-class, I guess." Everyone who is not actually rolling in the gutter will make this self-assessment. It usually means they have a mortgage.

Owning your own home is America's unique recipe for avoiding revolution and promoting pseudo-equality at the same time. To keep citizens puttering in their yards instead of sputtering on the barricades, the government has gladly deprived itself of billions in tax revenues by letting home "owners" deduct mortgage interest payments. By favoring housing over industry in access to capital we have deprived industry, the employer of our blue-collar squirearchy, of the money to expand and compete with foreign countries. The consequent flight to superior foreign products and cheaper foreign labor has led to unemployment here, and the bizarre, only-in-America spectacle of the jobless workingman sitting in his "own home" fuming at the thought that a "middle-class" person like himself should be in such straits.

The democratization of the law has given us the Tort Mystique. I am the only menopausal kid on the block who isn't going to law school; the Harvard hotshot has turned into the Harvard hot flash. A few years ago *Ms.* magazine ran a pathetic letter from a fifty-six-year-old woman who was attending first-year law school at night. Being a lawyer is now a "re-entry" job for older women and a sexy job for spring chickens, like the Catherine Hicks character in *Valley of the Dolls: 1981* who flounced and wriggled and tumbled into bed with James Coburn while the camera picked up her brief case lying on the coffee table with the half-finished martinis.

Familiarity breeds contempt not only between individuals but between citizens and their institutions. If too many people have too many dealings with the courts, the judicial system loses the majesty it must have in order to function as a restraining force. Such exclusivity benefits the social order by providing a natural protection for the Great American Family that everyone is trying to save. Ordinary people used to be prevented from divorcing, not only by the cost of lawsuits but by their abject fear of lawyers and courts. These were the stamping grounds of their betters and they shrank from them, choosing to put up with a difficult spouse rather than enter those dark, wood-paneled offices where, they were sure, they would be patronized by someone who looked and sounded like Claude Rains.

Now the floodgates have been opened and the veil has been removed. Television is full of lawyers and most of them are naked. The word is out: lawyers are just plain folks, and everybody's gotta right to go to court and sue hell out of everybody else.

If these litigious egalitarians want to win their cases,

they had better choose carefully from among newly minted women lawyers. The Tort Mystique is predicated on the *idée fixe* that law school is the place to go to learn how to be logical and how to argue. This attitude has resulted in a dismaying number of women who look upon the study of law primarily as a vanishing cream to remove those age-old female blemishes of emotionalism and unassertiveness.

The democratization of discrimination sounds strange but remember, we're talking about America. On October 15, 1983, the *New York Times* ran a story about a conference on the Italian experience in America headlined "SCHOLARS FIND BAD IMAGE STILL PLAGUES U.S. ITALIANS." Humbert S. Nelli, professor of history at the University of Kentucky, told his fellow scholars that although "the stigma of criminal activity" is still a problem, "the stigma may disappear as members of other groups take over criminal activities." After planting the seed of sawed-off affirmative action, Nelli went on to rhapsodize about his vision of the future "when Americans will look back nostalgically to the syndicate, as we look back now to the gunfighters of the Old West." Time-Life Books, take note.

We have democratized the intellectual process itself. Recently while browsing in a secondhand bookstore I bought a paperback copy of *The Intellectual and the City*, but I was unable to read it. When I got home I discovered that the original owner had highlighted the entire book—literally. Every line on every page had been drawn through with a bright green Magic Marker. It was a terrifying example of a mind that had lost all power of discrimination.

We tried to democratize fame but it backfired. The television talk show is carefully crafted around a casual living-room format designed to bring celebrities down from Olympus and show them relaxing and chatting together like just plain folks. It sounds cozy but there's a catch. Television's early stated intention to "come into our homes" has succeeded beyond anyone's wildest dreams.

The sensation that the celebrities are actually present makes the necessarily silent viewers feel like duds, the shy people who get left out of conversations, and triggers in them an emotion that Christopher Sykes identified in his biography of Lady Nancy Astor: "There is among the famous a freemasonry that offends the obscure."

The offense taken has led to outlandish efforts to get into *The Guinness Book of World Records* by performing such feats as eating five miles of spaghetti in three minutes to prove that everybody's gotta right to be famous.

The democratization of the femme fatale can be laid squarely at the feet of *Cosmopolitan* magazine, which stands in relation to true seductiveness as Robespierre to the *ancien régime*.

We may end up spreading the wealth but we will never spread the "It." Two women we have lately come to regard as femmes fatales are actually That Cosmo Girl. The bona fide femme fatale takes her leaf from the cry of Marlowe's Faust, "Her lips suck forth my soul." Donna Rice's stabs at sultriness come straight out of "Ten Ways to Look Sexy While Waiting in Line."

Bedding down was not an issue in Fawn Hall's case but her Cosmo Girl credentials are flawless. You *can* be sexy *and* successful! Work is sexy! Offices are sexy! Overtime is sexy! Shredding machines are sexy! "The Dedicated Man And *You*! Can You Stick By Him In A *Crisis*?"

Listening to Rice whining about the rigors of celebrity ("Everybody wants a piece of me") and Hall rotely reciting her endless job description, we heard not the hiss of the serpent of the Nile but Helen Gurley Brown's deathless exhortation to the daughters of the Common Man: "If you're a little mouseburger, come with me. I was a mouseburger and I will help you."

Would you believe the democratization of Lesbianism? Until the mid-seventies, the traditional or classic Lesbian was always a spinster and often a tweedy intellectual, with a stark glamour that titillated men and women alike. This is the woman that feminists destroyed when they pressured the media for "positive images" of Lesbians.

Suddenly open enrollment struck the Sapphic elite and dykes-for-the-masses were everywhere. We got the Lesbian detective, the Lesbian ghost, the Lesbian vampire, the possessed Lesbian, the Lesbian next door, the Lesbian with a heart of gold, the kept Lesbian, the other Lesbian, the Lesbian amnesiac, the Lesbian with cancer, and just plain Butch.

Could it get worse? Yes. We also got the Jason's Mommy Lesbian.

After her divorce, Jason's Mommy not only discovered her own potential but some other woman's as well. Having between them enough children to start a kindergarten, they decided to live together and practice family values. Mrs. Wiggs of the Cabbage Patch was into cunnilingus.

When some member of the big bad Establishment threatened this happy home with a pink slip or an eviction notice, the whole ménage went on television to explain their side of the story. The children always stole the show. As the loathsome little Jason raced up and down the aisles, the studio audience got the soothing idea that Jason's Mommy and her girlfriend were no more able to make love in peace than any bona fide married couple. By the end of the show they seemed so normal and heterosexual that the audience could almost forget they were Lesbians. To leave daytime-television fans smiling through their tears, little Jason was given the last word, piping the fadeout with "Mommy and Aunt Betty love each other."

A bold matriarchy, their country's pride, when once unleashed, can never be denied. The classic Lesbian is no more. In the name of equality, feminists rolled her up in her tweeds, weighted her with her scholarly tomes, and threw her overboard. The last thing she heard was "Everybody's gotta right to be a Lesbian."

The democratization of Lesbianism is fraught with danger.

There was once a time when Lesbians went scot-free in a homophobic world. All the rancor was reserved for homosexual men; Lesbians were regarded simply as nice maiden ladies with lots of dogs who shared a home for reasons of safety and thrift.

Most people guessed the truth on a subconscious level but they didn't feel threatened. Lesbianism has always been very soothing to the heterosexual majority for three reasons. First, Lesbians do not lust after little girls as some homosexual men lust after little boys. Second, because women are more class-conscious than men and have more to fear from a sexual encounter with trash, Lesbians do not go slumming. Third, female vanity being what it is, Lesbians do not chase spring chickens—no woman of fifty is going to undress in front of a woman of twenty no matter how much she might desire her.

These behavior patterns make the average Lesbian relationship suffocatingly stable, which in turn makes the participants hands-down favorites of landlords and neighbors, who appreciate the stability so much that they gladly put up with all the dogs.

As if the foregoing were not blessing enough, even the Far Right likes Lesbians. The November 1971 issue of the John Birch Society magazine, *American Opinion*, contains an article called "Sex Denied: Perversion and the Hatred of God" by Medford Evans. The article is a predictable attack on male homosexuality, but it contains a permissive, even good-natured reference to Lesbianism: "It seems to me natural enough for anybody to want to make love to a beautiful woman, including, imaginably, another woman."

No Lesbian in her right mind would blow this cover but radical-feminist Lesbians did when they started saying things like "Lesbianism is *now*! Lesbianism is an alternative acculturation within a resources-oriented framework of socialistic oneness!" (They forgot pussy.) These anarchistic fulminations chipped away at Lesbians' favored status as solid-citizen perverts who could do no wrong.

The Sapphic sisterhood got another boost in the early AIDS years when *Time* stated: "The disease is virtually unknown among Lesbians." This was followed by a funny letter to the editor from a man who wrote: "I am tired of hearing people say that AIDS is God's revenge on homosexuals. Using that logic, lesbians, among whom the disease is virtually unknown, must be God's chosen people."

Would the Radi-Clits blow their cover a second time? You bet. The January/February 1988 issue of *Visibilities*, a new Lesbian magazine published in New York, contains an incredible article insisting that Lesbians can *too* catch AIDS, just like the fellas. To prove that two women can draw blood in sex play, the author makes dubious but nonetheless nauseating references to "vaginal fisting" and "vampirism."

What will come of this equality if a real AIDS panic should take hold? The women in the Gay and Lesbian Alliance should ask themselves what they have to gain by joining forces with their increasingly castigated brothers. If AIDS were a disease linked to female homosexuality I seriously doubt that gay men would go out on a limb to help their sisters. To paraphrase a George Eliot character: "Men's men, straight or gay, they're much of a muchness." Politically active Lesbians would be wise to abandon the gay rights scene and revive the stereotype of the Doggy Ladies.

Chinks in America's egalitarian armor are not hard to find. Democracy is the fig leaf of elitism.

Equal opportunity is good, but inborn talent is better

as long as you don't say so out loud. Americans worship creativity the way they worship physical beauty—as a way of enjoying elitism without guilt: God did it.

Contempt for manual labor is a big factor in the shoddy manufacturing that has contributed to our trade imbalance. Only an American union leader would say, as Samuel Gompers did: "The promise of America for the laboring man is the promise of someday no longer having to work with his hands." If Mary McGrory's home repairmen are slapdash and surly, it's because they agree with him.

The happy many who own their own homes are the brahmins in that caste nightmare known as the American Dream. If America is suffering from a shortage of rental housing, it's because nobody wants to rent to renters. Checking the *own* block instead of the *rent* block on forms and applications is our way of dividing the wheat from the chaff. *Apartment* has become a dirty word; the few really nice buildings left strive for such euphemistic names as "towers" or "complex." The apartment dweller is one jump up from the trailer dweller and the gap is narrowing by the minute.

Everybody's gotta right to be a landed gent, so ruromania is back, if it ever left. "Lot" is out and "acreage" is in, "nearest neighbor" is in and "next-door neighbor" is out, and millions of white-collar Americans rationalize their purchase of a pickup truck by repeating "They're fun to drive" over and over until they believe it.

Ruromaniacs like to attribute their bucolic tic to their unquenchable pioneer spirit, but since we all know that Americans have less pioneer spirit than a Byzantine grand vizier, there must be another reason. The sage of the twenties, William Allen White, nailed it when he wrote: "Why are Americans so country-minded? We are Emporians all, because we desire to belong to the governing classes."

The accurate maxim, "the masses love a lord," has

found a cracked way to coexist with American democracy. Mother Nature being the first and most unyielding of aristocrats, we have set ourselves the task of preserving her shrinking peerage. The residents of a New England town get up at dawn to fuss over beached whales like ancient Hawaiian minions stoking a 400-pound queen. If a land developer with a roll of shopping mall blueprints under his arm had the misfortune to show up while these ichthyological obeisances are in full throttle, he might well be lynched. *Developer* and *growth* have become euphemisms for "too many people"; our pseudo-egalitarian closet misanthropes practice hatred of humanity and call it conservation.

We persist in believing that gambling is a gentleman's vice open only to people like Count Vronsky, who knew it was *comme il faut* to pay his gambling debts at once and let his tailor wait. Whenever state lotteries come under discussion, the tendency of poor people to spend too much on tickets invariably arises. The talk-show sages who regularly debate this issue sound like Victorian toffs mouthing hypocritical pieties about the "deserving poor" as opposed to the other kind. The crocodile tears shed by the "thoughtful" and "concerned" (Americanese for "the better sort") is actually a fear that some member of the undeserving poor might hit the jackpot and not know how to "handle" all that money.

America has a whole sheaf of unwritten sumptuary laws, but unlike ancient societies that told the poor what they couldn't wear, we tell the rich. People who would be terrified to joke about watermelons and pawnbrokers think nothing of making jokes about polyester. The last time I toured a book, three newspaper interviewers inserted snide references to my favorite pants suit into their stories. All three of these sumptuarists were women too young to remember having to iron satin slips and ten-gore circular skirts made of something called butcher linen, but like Cato the Elder ranting against centurions' wives in silk stolae, they would brook no excuses.

Uttering the word *class* out loud is most unwise but the published results of the endless surveys we take invariably manage to say it loud and clear. Anyone who wants to think like the elite—or pretend to when pollsters come around—need only study these upstairs-downstairs bulletins.

Pick a survey, any survey—say the one on attitudes toward breastfeeding done for the Healthy Mothers, Healthy Babies Coalition in Washington. I got this from one of those obscure little newspaper clippings that I file accordingly after a week or so of carrying them next to my heart in my polyester breast pocket:

> Support for breastfeeding varies with education and geography, the survey found. For example, only 44 percent of those with less than a ninth-grade education said working mothers can breast-feed, compared with 71 percent of college graduates. Support for breastfeeding among employed mothers was highest in the West, lowest in the South [read shack trash]. The strongest support for employer-provided breastfeeding facilities came from college graduates, men, single people, and those with incomes of more than $15,000 a year.

If you want to watch Americans throw democracy and equality to the winds and enshrine them at one and the same time, get tapped for jury duty and listen while one side eliminates Catholics who went to college and the other side eliminates Protestants who went to high school, until there's nobody left but twelve people incapable of understanding the case. That's the jury.

* * *

Thanks to "Democrazy," the so-called quality of life we hear so much about is best described with my angel mother's favorite expletive: It's a "double-asshole, shit sandwich, five-alarm turd sonofabitch."

If you agree but prefer to express yourself more loftily, you can say "I am an anti-Sharawaggist."

Sharawaggi is a Japanese word meaning irregular or asymmetrical. It entered European languages in the seventeenth century as a landscaping term to describe the kind of garden that the Age of Reason abhorred: wild, overgrown, undisciplined, "natural-looking"—the opposite of the sculptured gardens of Versailles.

In human terms, Sharawaggi was defined by Sir Harold Nicholson as "a dislike of correctness." In the Romantic Movement of the early nineteenth century, says Nicolson, Sharawaggi became a fad, not only in gardening but in etiquette and personal behavior—the Byronic version of "let it all hang out."

Sharawaggi has overtaken America. The idea that nobody is better than anybody else has given rise to the belief that it is impossible to give offense in a democratic society. The habit of personal restraint that marks civilized societies has been so thoroughly eroded by egalitarianism that we are coming to resemble revolutionary France as described by Norah Lofts: "Manners and morals had so far declined in the last ten years that theaters in poorer quarters had been obliged to post notices asking clients *de ne pas faire vos ordures dans les loges*."

The popularity of video tapes as well as the whole "couch potato" movement is directly related to a widespread reluctance to sit in a dark movie auditorium with the Sharawaggists while they yell and fart and carry on

loud conversations. At baseball games the "bleacher creatures" scream obscenities so loudly that it carries over into
radio and television sound, creating yet another free-
speech crisis that has rallied the midgets and dwarfs of the
American Civil Liberties Union to a defense of Shara-
waggist rights.

They might have rights but they don't have a way with
words. One of the most striking manifestations of Sharawaggi in today's life is the decline and fall of profanity. My
mother was a muleskinner cusser in the great tradition of
the U.S. Cavalry, capable of dazzling cascades and inge-
nious combinations, but the bleacher creatures' rotely
chanted repetitions of "fuck" demonstrate conclusively the
democratization of the foul mouth.

And then there's the full mouth. In both shows and
commercials, characters on television chew and talk with
their mouths open, suck on teeth, dig out lodged food with
a fingernail, and make lip-smacking noises that sound like
a cow trying to pull her foot out of a mud hole. They also
indulge in on-screen belching, ear digging, nose picking,
and scratching.

Once upon a time, back in the dear dead days before
everybody got "sensitive to the needs of others," teachers
like Miss Dove used to break children of these habits by
marking them down in a wonderfully subjective category
called "citizenship," but now we tolerate such actions without protest lest we be accused of setting arbitrary elitist
standards.

Kissing scenes are virtually indistinguishable from eating scenes. It's disgusting to look at wet tongues and listen
to slappy sounds, or to see a long band of spit stretching
from one mouth to the other like a suspension bridge
glistening in the dawn. The popularity of old black-and-
white movies may be due less to a chi-chi interest in "film
history" than to the reason that dare not speak its name:

the relief of knowing that the movie we are about to see was strictly censored.

Sharawaggi has also invaded politics. Someone is always getting briefed or de-briefed but fewer and fewer public figures know how to behave. During the Iran-Contra hearings, Representative Dante Fascell asked witness Robert McFarlane, on-camera, if he needed a "pit stop" before continuing his testimony. Bathroom humor is such an obvious and longstanding example of Sharawaggi that we need not dwell on it, but the Iran-Contra affair and the last few years in general have given us another: compulsive nicknaming.

Ollie North, Bud McFarlane, Cap Weinberger, Bob Schultz, Dick Secord, and Don Regan not only spoke of each other this way but were referred to as such in formal news broadcasts. Arkansas Representative Dale Bumpers, among many others, has referred to England's prime minister as Maggie Thatcher (which fits like Chuck De Gaulle), and Hugh Sidey of *Time* devoted an entire column to Librarian of Congress Dan Boorstin. Strangest of all was "Bob" Bork—so called even by those who loathed him.

In its purest sense, nicknaming is an elitist ritual practiced by those who cherish hierarchy. For preppies it's a smoke signal that allows Bunny to tell Pooky that they belong to the same tribe, while among good ole boys it serves the cause of masculine dominance by identifying Bear and Wrecker as Alpha males.

The current fad for political nicknaming is something very different from affectionate tags like Stonewall and Old Hickory, which are not precisely nicknames but noms de guerre or sobriquets. It is also different from the legacy of James Earl Carter, whose diminutive was more of a Southern quirk than an American trend. It is a war against dignity itself. In the race to Sharawaggi we have traded the backslap of the first name for the verbal goose of the nickname.

Correctness, or at least a yearning for it, is back if you look closely enough. I don't mean Miss Manners. She's an open advocate, and in America the real clues are always subliminal. I mean the Planters Peanuts commercials set in the 1920s.

There are two of them at this writing. The first shows a young father or uncle and a little boy of five or six at a baseball game. Both are wearing shirts and ties, and the man, like the other men around him in the grandstand, wears a visored cap like the one Robert Redford wore in *The Great Gatsby*.

The pair are like no father and son in any commercial with a contemporary setting. The man is thoughtful of the boy, asking "Can you see okay?" and "Want some peanuts?" but we sense that he is not frantically into fathering or worried about quality time. He has an *air* about him. As for the little boy, he's so polite and soft-spoken that he makes me forget my longstanding affinity for Good King Herod.

The other commercial shows a young mother with her son and daughter at the beach. Like the men in the background, the little boy wears a bathing suit with a top. Seeing the peanut vendor, he runs off as his mother calls out "Harry! Wait for your sister!" The little girl catches up and the two children race down the boardwalk, passing a starchy, gray-haired grande dame dressed in hat and gloves, with her handbag looped decorously over her wrist. In the background is a huge summer hotel where, we suspect, the grande dame is ensconced.

The commercials ostensibly aim for our taste buds by asking us to remember how good roasted peanuts were sixty years ago, but most viewers can't remember that far back. The purpose of these minidramas goes beyond conventional nostalgia. What they do is make us yearn for Planters Peanuts by making us yearn for the correctness of days gone by: the days when respectable people did not go out without a hat, the days when boys were expected to look after their sisters, the days of empathic fastidiousness when men were as self-conscious about their chest hair as women still are about their leg hair.

Subconsciously revolted by a long large dose of Anything Goes, Americans are flirting with inconvenience and discomfort. Fountain pens and men's suspenders have made a comeback; I would not be surprised to see a return to the straight razor and pants with button flies. Anti-Sharawaggists in increasing numbers are chomping at the bit to get at restraint.

9

THE AGE OF HUMAN ERROR

Last year a New York publishing house put the following notice in the trade journal *Publishers Weekly*.

> Harper & Row prides itself on the quality of its texts, but in a recent reorganization of the production department a crack developed into which OSCAR AND LUCINDA fell. As a result, many copyediting errors and omissions appear in the book which were discovered only after the book was already available for sale.
>
> We are now printing a corrected version of the text.... We are making every effort to supply wholesalers with this corrected text edition to assure our retail customers immediate access.
>
> Harper & Row will pay freight on the return of the defective first edition.... Harper & Row will pay freight on replacement orders and will honor the original purchase discount....
>
> All original editions of OSCAR AND LU-

CINDA remaining in our warehouse have been destroyed. Harper & Row sincerely regrets the inconvenience this problem might cause our customers and the disservice this has done to this very fine novel.

The same thing could have happened to one of my books. For the most part, copyeditors are free lancers who wander around New York working here, working there, with no central clearing house to separate the wheat from the chaff. A good copyeditor is a pearl beyond price and I have had the good fortune to cross paths with a couple, but as any writer will tell you, they are rare birds.

The copyeditor I drew was a brachycephalic, web-footed cretin who should have been in an institution learning how to make brooms. She had a tin ear and her initiative surfaced at all the wrong times. Finding my sentences too stark or unequivocal, she stuck in empty-calorie easements like "consider for a moment," and whenever she came to a particularly violent opinion, she softened it with "alas and alack," which sounds about as much like me as "goddamn sonofabitch" sounds like June Allyson. She changed my correct spelling and use of *empathic* to *emphatic*, confused *waspish* meaning *peevish* with the Anglo-Saxon meaning, completely missed and therefore "corrected" numerous puns and word plays, and for some reason that neither I nor anyone in my publisher's office could discern, every time I wrote *start*, she changed it to *begin*.

She had no sense of rhythm. I like to use as few commas as possible so that sentences will go down in one swallow without touching the sides, but she added so many commas that I ended up with syncopated indigestion on every page. Worst of all, she fiddled with a parody in which the order of words was the whole point of the exercise.

Besides being an idiot she was also a slob. Thanks to her erasures and different ink colors, the manuscript was a mess even before I started (began?) working on it. Going through a copyedited manuscript usually takes me a few hours, but I spent three solid days on that one. By the time I had corrected her corrections and restored my original sentences, it looked so awful that I refused to let my publisher send it to the printer, because authors have to pay for errors that we cause printers to make. The book was still on the disk so I reprinted the whole thing and copyedited the new manuscript myself.

Every field has occupational hazards and this story sounds like a writer's typical complaint. It is, but there's a larger issue here. Writers like larger issues. We like making connections, going from concrete to discrete and back again, tracing cause and effect, finding meanings in things. Even while I was cussing a blue streak and entertaining a fantasy of collaring the copyeditor in my publisher's office and beating the shit out of her in front of everybody, another part of my mind was working on what it all meant.

Here is what I concluded.

People are so busy dreaming the American Dream, fantasizing about what they *could* be or have a *right* to be, that they're all asleep at the switch. Consequently we are living in the Age of Human Error. Turn on the television news and the lead story will very likely be about what caused the latest wreck, crash, or act of war. It wasn't technology— no, indeed, that's doing fine. It was "human error."

This announcement is made with an air of relief, as if the anchorman were saying that things aren't so bad after all. We're all human, aren't we? Anybody can make mistakes, can't they? Nobody's perfect, right? The trail of this insidious logic is unmistakable if you know your America. Since we're all human, since anybody can make mistakes, since nobody's perfect, and since everybody is "equal," a human error is Democracy in Action.

How do we punish human error? We don't. How could

we, when the virtues of thoroughness, exactitude, and quest for perfection are now called obsessive-compulsive behavior, signs of a repressed personality instead of a good character? Besides, chewing people out involves a "value judgment"—an exercise in elitism and consequently forbidden. Worse, chewing people out is un-Nice Guy. Wallowing in an excess of "sensitivity to others," we let them resign instead of firing them, and then give them good recs because Nice Guys don't blacklist.

How do we excuse human error? Easy. The Human Erroroid has "problems"—an all-purpose American affliction that runs the gamut from affordable day care to low self-esteem.

I know nothing about day care, affordable or otherwise, but I can tell you something about self-esteem. While the copyediting mess was going on, I was having another battle with my landlord over the dirty entry and hallway of my building. It's a small-town, casual sort of place containing just four apartments, with none of the big-city amenities like janitorial service. The woman who used to clean it died some time ago, and in classic Southern fashion, the landlord never got around to hiring anybody else.

I kept complaining, and finally he got some woman to do it. I don't know where he found her, but the moment I set eyes on her I knew what was going to happen. She looked like one of those women who reads true confessions and goes around saying "The Lord will provide." Her bucket contained plain water from the spigot out back, which meant that it was cold, and there was no sign of soap or cleaning fluid in it, just a faint whiff of Clorox. She was using a dirty mop, and she herself looked dirty—the opposite of what Marines call "table pussy." In short, a case of low self-esteem.

I listened to her desultory swishing. Thanks to the screech of the front door, which needed oiling, I could tell that she did not go outside and change her water. When she had finished and gone, I went out and inspected her work. The hallway smelled sour, and she had missed entirely the two things I had complained specifically about: the grease on the edge of one step where somebody's garbage bag had dripped, and the banister railing that was sticky and disgusting to the touch.

After discussing the cleaning woman with a neighbor, who said, "I think she has problems," I called my landlord and offered him my deal: "You knock twenty-five dollars off my rent and I'll give you the cleanest goddamn building in Christendom." We agreed that I would scrub the hallway, entry, and banister once a month; and so, in the middle of the copyediting debacle, I went to work. When I finished, the smell of ammonia was so strong that the mailman had a sneezing fit, and later that day when the paper boy came to collect, he sneezed in my face.

The moral of this story encompasses not only the copyediting incident but the whole American festival of human error, Nice Guyism, and trendy people-to-people concepts. Self-esteem does not come from Self-Esteem Workshops, Self-Esteem Resources Centers, or Self-Esteem Crisis Hot Lines. Like all of life, self-esteem begins with one tiny seed.

If that slatternly woman who was hired to clean the building had done a spit-and-polish perfect job of it, she would have felt a little better about herself. Not much, maybe, but a little. That's how it starts. If the copyeditor had done such a good job on the book that I had written her a thank-you note, as I always do when I'm pleased, she would have felt good about herself.

When I finished scrubbing that hallway and stood there inhaling the clean smell and looking at the sun dance over the gleaming tiles, I felt *great* about myself—in the midst of a potentially disastrous publishing crisis that could have damaged my reputation as a writer, I was proud of being such a good janitress.

The "secret" of self-esteem is no secret at all. It is contained in Robert E. Lee's farewell to his troops after the surrender at Appomattox: "You will take with you the satisfaction that proceeds from a knowledge of duty faithfully performed."

10

Time has lost all meaning in that nightmare alley of the Western world known as the American mind. We wallow in nostalgia but manage to get it all wrong. True nostalgia is an ephemeral composition of disjointed memories—a tremulous attraction here, a perfect Christmas there, the smell of October in some forgotten year—but American-style nostalgia is about as ephemeral as copyrighted déjà vu.

What other people could take the very symbol of eternity—reincarnation—and turn it into the latest thing? During that particular fad we gorged ourselves on *The Reincarnation of Peter Proud, Carrie, The Other*, and any number of Damon-the-Demon, Owen-the-Omen spin-offs. A kid, plus reincarnation: the perfect American combo celebrating endless youth and life without death.

No American can avoid the national disease of "decaditis"—I indulge in it in this book. We type people according to the decade that matches their personality. The uptight are very fifties, nonconformists are very sixties, the self-absorbed are "coming from" the seventies. No sooner is a decade over than we start waxing nostalgic about it, no matter how bad it was. Our practice of zeroing in on the past so we can hurry up and talk about it makes me feel as if I were trapped in a batty time capsule with a bevy of ancient Romans who keep saying "Boy, this decline and fall is really something, isn't it?"

Fiddling with the past is a sign of deep national stress, like the Brumaire and Thermidor nonsense that grew out of the French Revolution when the Jacobins renamed the months. Confident people are relaxed about the past. Consider that intriguing dodge favored by Victorian novelists:

"In the spring of 18—, Lord Devon called on the vicar."

Or the Sir Walter Scott sentence:

"When the reign of the Plantagenet Lion still shimmered in the noonday sun. . . ."

Richard the Lionheart reigned from 1189-1199, a nice neat decade, but neither Scott nor his readers felt obligated to arrange themselves for the convenience of people who make miniseries like "Call To Glory," whose whole point was a slavish obeisance to the sixties. They could afford to be vague about dates because they enjoyed a healthy sense of participation in the national continuity celebrated by such novels. By contrast, Americans must get what we can out of the Lesley-Ann Down, Harrison Ford movie blurbed "Love hasn't been like this since 1943!"

Americans have regularly fallen victim to the disease of decade loyalty. Our foremost casualty was F. Scott Fitzgerald, troubadour of the twenties, whose adherence to the Flaming Youth lifestyle that he recorded killed him at forty-four. Another casualty is that stormy petrel of the New Deal known as the "little old lady in tennis shoes" who never got out of the thirties. Today's yuppies, whose materialism would go unnoticed had they not been hippies first, acquired the habit of going to extremes in the sixties, the decade they cannot shake off.

The latest victim of America's time warp is Nancy Reagan, who has made it obsessively clear that she wants her husband to have "a place in history."

Okay, babe, here it is:

"Ladies and gentlemen, the Paradigm of the United States."

P: Well, my opening statement is with regard to the annexation of Schleswig-Holstein. I was awakened at four this morning to take a call from our ambassador in Copenhagen, who asked not to be identified. He informed me that King Frederick VII of Denmark has seized the German-speaking Danish duchy of Schleswig and the Danish-speaking German duchy of Holstein. The king justified this dastardly act on the grounds that he is Duke *of* Schleswig and Holstein even though the Almanach de Gotha lists him as Duke *in* Schleswig and Holstein. America's vital interests are clearly at state, so I have dispatched Fort Bragg. Now I'll take questions. Sam? No, you forgot your red dress. Helen?

Q: Mr. Paradigm, isn't there more to the Schleswig-Holstein question than the dispute over the duke's title?

P: You know, I'd like to share with you something Margaret Thatcher told me. She said only three people have ever understood what the annexation of Schleswig-Holstein is all about. One was Prince Albert, who died at forty-four. The second was a Heidelberg professor who went mad, and the third was Lord Palmerston, who said he forgot whatever it was that he understood. It's a troubled land. Sam?

Q: Sir, what American interests are there in Schleswig-Holstein that could possibly justify the deployment of so many troops?

P: They're not troops, they're a presence. To counteract the force.

Q: What force, sir?

P: The evil force. It's everywhere. That's why we have a presence in Llanfairpwllgwngllgogferychywll. Vice Paradigm Bush toured it last week wearing a leek deflector. Afterwards he called me and said we're not going to let a cowardly bunch of force change America's policy with regard to the wars of Edward the First.

Q: Mr. Paradigm, what is the force up to in Schleswig-Holstein?

P: The same thing it's up to in Bosnia-Herzegovina—the destabililization of political parties. As you know, these consist of the Progressive Conservative Liberals, the Constitutional Reactionary Democrats, the Counterinsurgent Anti-Revolutionary Republican Royalists, the Anti-Clerical Revisionist Moderate Socialists, the Neocapitalist Reform Syndicalists, and the Doltz. The force is trying to turn them into warring factions.

Q: Mr. Paradigm, is the force behind Holstein's anti-woman declaration?

P: Well, Sarah, I've never heard of any anti-woman declaration with regard to Holstein.

Q: You have so. It's been on your desk for eight hundred years. It's called the Salic Law and it says that no country in the Holy Roman Empire can have a woman king.

P: Sarah, we're going to have an X-rated force here in a minute.

Q: You know what I'm talking about. Frederick VII doesn't have any children. When he dies, Prince Christian of Glucksberg is going to claim the Danish throne on the grounds that he married Frederick's cousin. Holstein still considers itself part of the Holy Roman Empire, and they said they won't accept a king who goes through a woman. What are you going to do about that?

P: We're doing everything we can.

Q: Mr. Paradigm, what is America's role in the Holy Roman Empire?

115

P: The same role we're playing in the War of Jenkins's Ear. Peacekeeping.

Q: Sir, many people fear that our involvement in the War of Jenkins's Ear is going to become 'another Punic.'

P: Oh, I wouldn't say that. Our commitment in the Punic War was to guarantee safe passage across the Alps for Hannibal's elephants. Jenkins's Ear is a lot smaller.

Q: Mr. Paradigm, why should America care that a Spanish pirate cut off an English naval officer's ear? What's the clear and present danger in that?

P: Escalation. Vice Paradigm Bush toured Captain Jenkins's ship wearing a steel-lined. . . . Well, I guess I'll take another question.

Q: Mr. Paradigm, the Elector of Saxony has taken advantage of the confusion surrounding the War of Jenkins's Ear to have himself crowned King of Poland with the support of Russia and Austria, over the objections of Spain, which has threatened to declare war on Italy for the return of the duchy of Tuscany now held by Austria, which is demanding that France cede Lorraine to Prussia in exchange for making Don Carlos king of Naples and Sicily. Do you foresee our involvement in this?

P: You bet. That's what America's all about. If you want to be a peacekeeper and Mary Queen of Scots isn't available, always look for an Elector of Saxony.

Q: Sir, is there any truth to the rumor that Queen Draga of Serbia was defenestrated?

P: I'm not going to get into that. As far as this administration is concerned, she was thrown out the window.

Q: Mr. Paradigm, there seems to be some confusion about our involvement in the attempted flight of Louis the Sixteenth and Marie Antoinette from revolutionary Paris. Yesterday Secretary Schultz said we helped them escape, but this morning White House Chief of Staff Howard Baker said we helped capture them. Who's lying?

P: Nobody. We wanted to be fair to both sides, so Bob planned their escape and Howard planned their capture.

Q: Mr. Paradigm, if we could move on to domestic matters. Now that Thomas De Quincey, Samuel Taylor Coleridge, and Edgar Allan Poe have all been forced to resign as chairman of the Just Say No To Drugs Commission, who's the next candidate on Ed Meese's list?

P: You know, I'd like to share with you something that the first Eskimo graduate of West Point said as he lay wounded at Marathon. "Wherever there's a force, I'll be there. Wherever there's a faction, I'll be there. Wherever there's an archduke beatin' up a count, I'll be there. You might never see me again but you'll be hearin' about me 'cause I just signed up as a non-combat advisor to Vercingetorix the Gaul."

Well, God bless America, and God bless us every one. "Thank you, Mr. Paradigm."

11

THE COLOR PURPLE: WHY I AM A ROYALIST

I felt as if the world had come to an end on that hot April day in 1945 when the announcer broke into "Tom Mix" with the news that Roosevelt was dead.

I was home with Granny and Jensy, our cleaning woman. We stared at each other in mute shock, then did what apartment dwellers all over America were doing at that moment: we ran out into the hall.

It was near dinnertime; all the neighbor women had been cooking and their floured hands looked like white gloves. While we were huddled together in the hall, Mama returned from the grocery store. Granny had discovered that we were out of pepper and sent her to buy some. Usually when she had a small package she could not resist tossing it in the air, but this time her tomboyish swagger had deserted her. She held the little bag at her side in an uncharacteristically sedate way, behaving for once like the perfect Southern lady of Granny's dreams. She looked at the weeping women and spoke in a flat voice.

"Now that little hick is president."

No one had thought of Truman until now. The mention of his name provoked exclamations of despair and fear that rose up like a collective moan. Orderly transition meant nothing to the crowd in the hallway; in those first shocked moments, Harry Truman was not the vice president but a usurper.

Being reminded of small-town men who wore stetsons and spoke in rural accents was all Jensy needed. She screamed and fainted. Everyone ran for ice. They worked over her, fanning, patting, and pulling her arms up over her head until she came to. We got her back into our apartment and helped her to the sofa; Mama moved the electric fan to the table beside her and I got her a glass of water. The radio was still on, playing "Swing Low, Sweet Chariot." Looking out the window, I saw a streetcar motorman put his head down on the controls and sob. Across the street, the Chinese man who ran the laundry stood in front of his shop, gripping his elbows as though longing for the comfort of an ancestral garment in which to hide his hands.

Herb came home. Always stoic, he was now more so. Clearing his throat, he spoke with difficulty.

"I think we should drink a toast to Mr. Roosevelt." Glancing at Jensy's tear-streaked face, his remote British features softened. "How about a whiskey collins, old girl?"

She drew herself up in outraged virtue. "Mr. King, you knows me better den dat. Whiskey give you a purple nose, a green liver, a red eye, a black heart, an' it put a yeller streak right up de middle of yo' back. Jes' bring me a glass of mix widout de motion."

We relaxed; she sounded like her old self again. Herb fixed three whiskey collinses, a frosty glass of lemon juice,

119

soda, and sugar for Jensy, and ginger ale with a dash of sherry for me. We raised our glasses.

"He was a gentleman," said Herb.

"Quality," Jensy agreed, blowing her nose. "Dat new l'il peckerwood ain't."

"He sold shirts!" Granny trumpeted.

We drove Jensy home. Lately she had been complaining about the trash who neither sowed nor reaped who were ruining her neighborhood and giving respectable colored people a bad name. But on this night the Sodomites, Jezebels and Satan's limbs of her tirades were nowhere in sight. The street was deserted; decorum reigned everywhere on April 12, 1945, the day that women cooked in white gloves.

I am a member of the only generation of Americans since 1776 to have experienced something very close to the permanence and psychological security of monarchy.

Adults regarded the New Deal as the heyday of the Common Man, but we children of the thirties cut our teeth on absolutism. Like Addie Pray in *Paper Moon*, our imaginations were fired by this "Frankie Roosevelt" who did so many magical things. It was obvious that he was eternal and immortal because he had been president for as long as we could remember, so long that the words "president" and "Roosevelt" ran together like the "Now-Ilaymedowntosleep" that we rattled off each night. Because we became aware of him while we were in the fairy tale stage, it was easy to believe that his voice floating out of the radio was like the royal touch that banished evil and restored happiness. Easy, too, to transform his "Martin, Barton, and Fish" into a litany that made us nod three times as we rolled church and state together into one soft bed.

120

The modus operandi variously attributed to Jesuits and totalitarian governments—"Give me a child until he is seven and he is mine forever"—also applies to Roosevelt babies. At least to this one. I can't take another election; I'm ready for an American monarchy.

The people who can be counted on to disagree with me most violently are those who devour supermarket newspapers about Charles and Di, Andrew and Fergie, and the alleged meeting between the ghost of Princess Grace and the ghost of Elvis the King.

My enemies on the other side of the socio-economic fence are the left-leaning liberal intelligentsia who unplugged their phones during "Upstairs, Downstairs" and videotaped "Fall of Eagles" so they could follow the fortunes of Bertie, Alix, Nicky, Vicky, Dicky, Willy, Fritz, and Sasha. Would the Kaiser's withered arm give him an inferiority complex? Was Elisabeth of Austria going to have a nervous breakdown over Rudolph's suicide? How much did Alix know about Bertie's affairs?

Americans are the Uriah Heeps of democracy, wringing our hands over equal rights from the depths of a purple velvet closet. Though few will admit it, in many ways we already have a monarchy. The fanfare surrounding our summit conferences recalls Henry VIII and Philip of France meeting on the Field of the Cloth of Gold. We crowned the world's last czar—of energy—and our lust for titles is so consuming that, alone of all nations, we let our politicians retain elective and appointive titles after leaving office: Joseph P. Kennedy was called "Ambassador" for the rest of his life even though he served only three years in London.

The itch to crown someone, if only a Corn Harvest Queen, pervades our populist heartland. Our street gangs are Dukes, our marauding businessmen are Barons, and the favorite headline word in women's publications is Milady. Our television talk shows resemble court *levées*; we have turned *People* magazine into our very own *Debrett's Peerage*, and we invade the privacy of public figures like courtiers crowding into Louis XIV's bedchamber as he sat on the royal pot.

The celebrity look-alike craze a few years ago had all the earmarks of the medieval changeling myth. Ostensibly in the name of feminism, complex marriage contracts fit for the Landgravin of Hesse-Darmstadt have replaced the hope chest in the hearts and minds of American brides. The historical novel is back, more Sir-stuffed and Lord-laden than ever, and we have fallen so in love with the aristocratic ideal of heroism that we attribute it to absolutely anybody: the mentally retarded housewife with cancer of the feet who enters a jogging marathon is received as Boadicea.

The most glaring examples of our closet royalism involve the occupants of the White House. Our president is the world's only democratically elected head of state who has his own personal anthem, with lyrics by that foremost champion of heraldic pageantry, Sir Walter Scott. "Hail to the Chief" is from Canto II of "The Lady of the Lake."

Every other democracy calls its leader's wife "Mrs." but we call ours "First Lady," a rarefied appellation borrowed from British royal etiquette that goes back to medieval times. When the king is unmarried and there is no Queen Dowager (his mother) and no Princess Royal (his oldest sister), the wife of the oldest Royal Duke (the King's brother) becomes the ranking woman of the realm. Because she goes first in processions and receives other perquisites normally enjoyed by a Queen Consort, she is designated "First Lady of England." Designated, not called; having at least one and probably several titles to begin with, she does not, like her ostensibly egalitarian White House counterpart, crave another.

Forced to elect our presidents, we do our best to ennoble their children. John Van Buren returned home from a visit to England to find himself dubbed "Prince John" merely because he had danced with the young Princess Victoria. We called Teddy Roosevelt's daughter "Princess Alice," but the fun really started in her cousin Franklin's administration.

Following the scrapes of Royal Dukes has always been a favorite pastime of bona fide subjects. The English were mightily entertained by the seven dissipated sons of George III, who sold army commissions and tortured their valets. Not to be outdone, and willing to make do with anything, New Deal Americans kept tabs on the traffic tickets amassed by Jimmy, Elliott, Franklin Jr., and John. As time went on, tracking the marriages, divorces, and preppily named offspring of the Roosevelt sons and their sister Anna became a national obsession; Depression-era Americans sounded like gouty squires poring over a stud book as they discussed the lineage of the various Sistys and Buzzys who swarmed through the decade of the Common Man.

The royalist excesses of the Kennedy years are too familiar to list, except to note that the most startling addition to the national vocabulary accrued not to a Kennedy but to Vice President Lyndon B. Johnson: suddenly a large Texas ranch was called a *fief*.

Richard Nixon gave us some respite from our dirty little secret by forging an "imperial presidency" that we could criticize in self-righteous democratic tones, but he stuck us with an unelected successor like a Roman emperor adopting a nephew. When the nephew announced the self-evident truth, "I'm a Ford, not a Lincoln," we relaxed, secure in the knowledge that we really were an egalitarian democracy after all. But two years later, something terrible happened.

Enter the House of Hookworm. Jimmy and Rosalynn served up a Nicholas-and-Alexandra marriage; Brother Billy was the regicide Philippe Egalité; Sister Ruth the preacherwoman was Cardinal Richelieu; Gloria's star-

123

crossed son languishing in prison supplied a Stuart touch; Miz Lillian was Franz Josef's mother, Archduchess Sophie, who was known as "the only man the Hapsburgs ever produced"; and little Amy was a horse-faced Infanta straight out of the *Almanach de Gotha*.

The Carters marked a turning point in our closet royalism. At long last we were forced to admit that God made too many common people, so we elected Ronald Reagan and turned our attention to the royal wedding of the Prince and Princess of Wales. It was just the fix we needed; Princess Diana's intimate response on this occasion is not known, but July 29, 1981 was the day that everybody in America had an orgasm, even Jane Pauley.

Now that we are tired, poor, huddled, and here, what are the chances of someday having a monarchy of our own?

The biggest stumbling block is our fear of an Established church. You can't have a monarchy without an Established church because you can't have a coronation without one. The problem is one of holy oils. An unanointed monarch is invalid and viewed as a pretender to the throne, yet only three faiths—Roman Catholic, Eastern Orthodox Catholic, and Anglican—have holy oils.

What do do? A greasy king being better than no king at all, the American monarchist is tempted to suggest that all three oleaginous faiths conduct a tripartite coronation. But this solution is fraught with danger. Americans are terrified of leaving any religion out of things, so we would have to have an ecumenical coronation that included representatives from every creed, oily or not, practiced in the land.

There is no telling where it would end, or if it would ever end except in the death of the monarch. By the time he was Born Again, Circumcised Again, held underwater, and forced to play with rattlesnakes, we would find that we had once again snatched self-defeat from the jaws of compromise.

Vexing problems such as this aside, hereditary monarchy offers numerous advantages for America. It is the only form of government able to unify a heterogeneous people. Thanks to centuries of dynastic marriage, the family tree of every royal house is an ethnic grab bag with something for everybody. We need this badly; America is the only country in the world where you can suffer culture shock without leaving home. We can't go on much longer depending upon disasters like Pearl Harbor and the Iranian hostage-taking to "bring us together."

Some American monarchists have suggested offering the crown to a descendant of the Adams or James families, but that would only perpetuate the Wasp hegemony that so many resent. A better solution is the time-honored practice of inviting someone from another country to take the crown. Importing a descendant of one of the European royal houses would give us a polyglot prince with an inborn capacity for traveling well. If, for example, we put a Stuart on our throne, ethnic Catholics, Lost Cause Southerners, and readers of *When Bad Things Happen to Good People* could all identify with him.

Hereditary monarchy would put an end to the politics of Nice Guyism. Richard Nixon's royal counterpart, Louis XI of France, was called the "Spider King" both for his pot belly and spindly legs, as well as for his habit of lurking motionless in windows to spy on people. Louis repelled everyone; even his wetnurse quit, saying "There's something about that baby I don't like." All he had going for him was a brilliant mind. With no need to make himself pleasant to voters, he was able to devote all of his mental and physical energies to the task of governing. Today he is acknowledged as one of France's best kings and one of history's foremost administrative geniuses. Eavesdropping, list-making, misanthropic, paranoid insomniacs do things right if they're let alone, but the strain of pretending to like people will destroy them every time. (I know, I've been on four book tours).

A nation of hypochrondriacs is fit only for a king. Hereditary monarchy would punch up the American disease scene. Late-night public service announcements could dwell on gout and scrofula, and Jerry Lewis would be so busy doing telethons for Capet foreskin and Hapsburg jaw that we would never again have to look at a cute crippled kid.

Hereditary monarchs are unsurpassed as patrons of the arts because every monarch wants his reign to be called the Age of Himself. Culture piped through great vanity emerges as great culture, but a just-folks president must hold the pillar of the church dearer than the flying buttress and pretend to be content with Zane Grey. The pretense seldom strains credulity.

Finally and most important, hereditary monarchy would please feminists by putting the arrogant medical profession in its place. No one is impressed with the title "Doctor" when real titles like Duke, Marquess, Earl, Viscount, and Baron abound.

Aside from knee-jerk bleatings about the inherent political genius of the People, the leading objection to hereditary monarchy is hereditary insanity. Americans have imbibed the idea that all monarchs are sadistic maniacs who pop off and commit bloodcurdling deeds, like the night Catherine de Medici invited France's Protestant leaders to dinner and had them murdered at the table. The massacre of St. Bartholomew's Day was a bit much, but at least it was livelier than White House prayer breakfasts.

Because madness and horror make the best novels and movies, it is all too easy to forget that more monarchs than not have borne sobriquets like the Good, the Wise, the Well-Beloved, and the Green Gallant. In any case, I would much rather be at the mercy of someone with the power to say "Off with her head!" than be nibbled to death by a bureaucratic duck. Kings and queens might do wicked things but they don't nag. One thing I like about Bloody Mary: she never said a word about lung cancer.

12

TWO KIDNEYS IN TRANSPLANT TIME

I am afraid of organs. Make that "organ-afraid" in honor of our hyphen-obsessed times. I am also transplant-afraid. In fact, I don't like anything about this whole switcheroo business.

Many people feel the same way but are loath to say so because organs are all tied up with America's twin gods, Compassion 'n' Humanitarianism. We're supposed to be organ-positive, but I am organ-negative and not at all loath to say so.

My fears are not triggered by the plethora of information about organs ("organ awareness") with which we are bombarded because I don't understand medical matters, but I understand all too well the Orwellian phraseology the experts slip into when they get going on the subject.

Take, for example, that sentence we hear so often: "A

donor heart was located and flown to the hospital." The rational part of my mind knows what this means: one set of doctors removed the heart of someone who just died and rushed it to the sick patient who needed it so that another set of doctors could perform a modern, miraculous transplant operation.

So much for the rational part of my mind. But what of the other part? The American part: that ghoul-haunted woodland of Weir, that dank tarn of Auber wherein dwell the spectral tendrils of egalitarian mist? This is the part that tells me George Orwell was right when he said that bad English is the beginning of the end.

Note the two passive verbs in our sentence: "was located" and "[was] flown." The passive voice is the voice of Sneaky Pete. Now look at the noun used as an adjective: "donor" heart. People who tailor words to suit their own needs will tailor anything to suit their own needs. The originator of that "donor heart" phrase *snatched* the noun out of its proper place and *put it in* where it was needed. See what I'm getting at?

At this point I should write that familiar qualifying sentence that begins: "Of course, I am not implying. . . ." But I am implying. Not only am I implying, I am saying flat out that I am worried (make that "concerned") that somebody out there in Democracyland is getting ready to render some of us organ-free for the benefit of the organ-deprived.

I keep a file of transplantese that I take out and read every now and then, the way a normal woman my age reads old love letters. Among my favorite clippings is one from the *Washington Times* dated June 18, 1982, headlined "MOUSE BRAIN TRANSPLANT SUCCESSFUL." It says:

SAN FRANCISCO—A piece of brain has been successfully transplanted from one mouse into another, where it not only survived but correctly

129

hooked itself up and functioned near normally, a scientist reports. "This is what I call my science fiction experiment—except that it works," said Dr. Dorothy T. Krieger, chief of endrocrinology at Mount Sinai Medical Center in New York City.

How do you like them droppings? I suppose the discrepancy between the San Francisco dateline and the New York (make that "New York-based") doctor is no cause for alarm. Perhaps Dr. Krieger was interviewed while attending a convention, or better yet, took a well-earned vacation from her tiny labors in the city of mislaid hearts.

Much more disturbing is what comes next:

Although the partial brain transplant succeeded in seven out of eight tries with mice, Ms.[sic] Krieger said, "I will make no speculation as to any possible relation of this procedure to humans. I wouldn't touch that with a 10-foot pole . . . This is only the first experiment."

Note the unclear slide from the writer's summation to the doctor's quotation in the sentence beginning "Although. . . ." Did the writer ask Dr. Krieger to speculate on the possibility of applying her procedure to humans, or did she bring up the subject herself? Somebody brought it up. And what do we make of her defensive reference to ten-foot poles? And what do those elliptic dots stand for? It all bodes ill in a country where "equality before the law" has been shortened to "equality."

Since experiments on mice are always done with human medicine in mind, we are justified in reflecting on Aulus Gellius's dictum, *Ex pede Herculem*: "From the foot alone we may infer Hercules."

The last paragraph of the mouse clipping says: "The research, the most dramatic ever done with such trans-

plants, is to be described this month in the British journal
Nature." I don't subscribe to the British journal *Nature* but
I do subscribe to the *Washington Post*. Imagine how urine-
dead I felt on September 19, 1983 when I found myself
staring at a five-column headline: "VA. DOCTOR PLANS COM-
PANY TO ARRANGE SALE OF HUMAN KIDNEYS."

The article is by *Post* staffer Margaret Engel, who really
knows how to write a riveting lead:

> The growing demand for human body parts has
> prompted a maverick Virginia doctor to establish
> a company, believed to be the first of its kind, that
> would broker human kidneys for sale by arranging
> for donors throughout the world to sell one of their
> kidneys.

The colorful Wild West word *maverick* describes Dr. H.
Barry Jacobs, "whose license to practice in Virginia was
revoked after a 1977 mail-fraud conviction involving Medicare and Medicaid." While this is not cheering, it doesn't
bother me too much because my fear awareness is not
white-collar-criminal-oriented: con men can be fun. However, the article goes on to say: "Jacobs, who served 10
months in jail for his 1977 conviction, said he now works
as a consultant in medical malpractice lawsuits." Check that
phrasing. Not he *is* a consultant, but he *said* he is. This is
turning into a fine kettle of fish on its way to becoming a
fine kettle of kidneys.

The piece goes on to describe the medical and legal
problems of Jacobs's projected plan. It is extremely long
and involved but fascinating nonetheless, for tucked here
and there amid the scientific and bureaucratic detail are
certain buzzwords and convoluted euphemisms guaranteed to give the America-wise reader a jolt.

"It will be pure, free choice on their part," Jacobs said
of the donors. Why did he feel it necessary to emphasize

131

this? He goes on to say that the motivation to sell their body parts "would be whatever motivates someone to sell: greed, bills."

Can't you hear it? "Hi! This is Pam at Friendly Credit Bureau. I've worked out a debt-consolidation plan for you."

The colorful maverick continues: "There will be proper, written informed consent. Since many potential donors can't read, it [the informed consent conference] will be tape-recorded." Written, yet tape-recorded, you see?

Now we come to some exposition by reporter Margaret Engel:

> Other health professionals active in transplant activities say they had feared the creation of such a venture and supported a bill introduced in August by U.S. Rep. Albert Gore (D-Tenn.) to prohibit the sale of human organs.

Note the phrase: "*Other health professionals active in transplant activities. . . .*" This is a perfect example of how the search for euphemism destroys a writer's ear. Using "active" and "activities" that close together creates a discord. Such a lapse tells me that a writer is concentrating on *not* saying something. Exactly who are these "health professionals"—doctors, nurses, technicians, candy stripers, Burke and Hare?—and what is the difference between transplant operations and transplant "activities?" If it's anything like the "shower activity" so active in weather reports, I want to know the exact definition of rain.

Now comes something that will make you feel red, white, and blue all over. Explaining Medicare's role in reimbursing hospitals for removing a donor's kidney, a spokesman for the Health Care Financing Administration said: "The cost of harvesting" is covered.

Harvesting . . . what a soothing euphemism for the land of Thomas Jefferson, who said "Those who labor in the earth are the chosen people of God." Or as Thomas Cowper put it: "God made the country, man made the town." Americans believe wholeheartedly in these maxims. If it's country it must be cool, so apply the rustic word *harvesting* to what that city boy Jack the Ripper did, and no one will remember that Jack the Ripper did it.

Back to reporter Engel's exposition: "The problem of the great demand and low supply of human organs is one that the federal government itself is trying to solve. . . ."

Yes, indeed. Can't you see the civics textbooks of the future? *Duties of the federal government: print the money, deliver the mail, declare war, and harvest kidneys.*

Next we hear from Surgeon General C. Everett Koop, who wants to keep the government out of the organ business. To this end, he called a meeting of medical officials to set up a privately funded foundation to encourage people to donate organs. Said a spokesman for Dr. Koop: "We're hoping that a leader will emerge."

They needn't worry. If the American hyphen-harvesters keep churning out Germanic compounds, it won't be long before we have one nation, one leader, and lots of kidneys.

Back to reporter Engel:

> . . . worldwide demand for such operations is expected to further overwhelm the meager supply. This inequity could lead to some organ-selling companies who might not take the proper medical and legal precautions in obtaining organs, some worry.

Some had better worry; this tactful paragraph translates into visions of the Mafia going into the kidney business.

Always leave 'em laughing, so the article ends with a statement by Dr. Harold Meryman, past president of the

American Association of Tissue Banks, who worries that the whole transplant movement will take an elitist turn: "Any millionaire with cirrhosis of the liver will gladly pay a half million dollars. That's not considered to be the American way."

Of course it's the American way, but that's not why I am organ-afraid. What worries me is that other American way, the one that is even more tempting than money. I have visions of a mad dash of Nice Guyism gone awry. The lugubrious pleas for a kidney here, a liver there, a heart in Sheboygan that descend like a sledgehammer on a neurotically friendly nation could easily inspire an organ Robin Hood to kill healthy people just to be able to arrive at the hospital in the nick of time with the needed part. When the melting imprimatur of Joan Lunden beckons, a line will form at the thorax.

Organ transplants have joined motherhood and apple pie on the list of things Americans must not be against. Well, tough titty—God knows whose—I'm against them. As Edgar Allan Poe said in the poem I ponied earlier: "But Psyche, uplifting her finger, said 'Sadly this star I mistrust.' "

The name of the poem is "Ulalume." You know what a *ulalume* is, don't you? It's the tiny gland that feeds the spleen, and I'm keeping mine.

13 UNSPORTIVE TRICKS

Junk mail used to look so obviously junky that we tossed it unopened into the trash or marked it "Return to Sender" and dropped it back in the box. But this cost the senders money—"dollars" in junk mailese—so they devised pitiless ways of tricking us into opening and reading it. Taking as their motto, "The only thing we have to use is fear itself," they decorated the front of their envelopes with messages calculated to scare us to death.

"URGENT! IMMEDIATE REPLY REQUESTED!" is on just about everything.

"OPEN THIS BEFORE YOU PULL OUT OF YOUR DRIVEWAY!" is from an auto insurance firm.

"WILL THIS BE OUR FINAL EPIDEMIC?" in rash-red letters next to your name is the inspiration of Physicians for Social Responsibility, who presumably decided to use the AIDS panic to get us to open their letters about nuclear war prevention.

"SUPPOSE SOLDIERS CAME AND TOOK YOUR SISTER AWAY IN A TRUCK?" asks Amnesty International. Not mother, not wife, not daughter, but that star boarder of the male id, the first virgin in his life, his sister—as in: "Would you want your sister to marry one?"

Junk mailers have also invented peekaboo greed. This is the window envelope containing a letter folded in such a way that an incomplete but intriguing sentence is visible above the recipient's name. Meant to look as if the letter was folded wrong by accident, the partial sentence reads: "Consideration and Compensation for Your Expense of Time and. . . ." No, it's not a check. The unfolded letter says that *if* we stay at one of the company's resorts, we will get discounts on items for sale there.

Then there is the official-looking envelope. This one is from the "Department of Verification" and has a Washington, D.C. return address and a seal of office. Have we inherited Montana or are we being billed for it? Neither. It's a letter verifying the recipient as an official buyer of discount items.

The smarmiest piece of junk mail—actually junque mail—comes in a starkly plain, pearl-gray envelope in whose lower left-hand corner sits a small but tasteful instruction.

OFFICIAL INVITATION
POSTMASTER: Please deliver as soon as possible.

It's from America's venerable secular abbey, the Smithsonian Institution. You've been invited to a party!

FLORENCE KING
You are one of a small group of
Purkins Corner Residents
invited to become National Associates
of the Smithsonian Institution.

They don't know that the only status symbol in Purkins Corner is buying whiskey by the fifth instead of by the

136

pint. The accompanying letter says that membership includes generous discounts on "reproductions"—doubtless that graven image of the pre-Columbian Incan caught in an eternal squat—and on something never before offered in junk mail: a dulcimer. The Renaissance comes to K-Mart. Ben Jonson hits I-95. Just leave a kiss within the Slurpee glass and I'll not ask for a peel-away sweepstakes coaster.

Loneliness is good for business, so junk mailers have devised ways to trick us into thinking that a solicitation is really a personal letter. Their favorite ploy is the envelope addressed by hand. The staffer chosen for this sadistic ruse has a loopy, immature penmanship designed to trigger memories of long-lost daughters or old friends from P.S. 31.

Ms. magazine uses a combination of loneliness and celebrity worship. On one of their subscription pitches they leave off the name of the magazine in the return address and substitute a stamp of Gloria Steinem's signature like a congressional frank gone awry to make recipients think they have received a personal communication from one of America's leading egalitarian Junkers.

The manager of Shell Oil's merchandising department writes whole letters by hand, using a simulacrum of lined notebook paper to suggest an intimacy so mellowed by time that standing on the slightest ceremony would be an insult. "Just a quick note to tell you that I discovered some really super items for you in my recent travels around the country," he begins, and gushes on for two printed pages.

The *American Spectator* simply lies to the lonely, typing the word *Personal* on the envelope and highlighting it with a yellow Magic Marker. Inside is one of the most incredible pitch letters ever penned, a four-page threnody about mounting costs from editor-in-chief R. Emmett Tyrrell Jr., who turns into a Jewish mother in the opening paragraph: *"It is 9:15 P.M. and I am alone here in an almost totally dark office."*

Leftwingers do it, too. American Civil Liberties Union Director Ira Glasser begins his pitch: *"It is late at night. I'm tired and my burning eyes are telling me it's time to quit."* It is, Ira, it is. Thanks to you and your gremlins, the U.S. Constitution has turned into Mr. Nice Guy's hankie.

The flip side of sadism is masochism, so if you wish to play the dominant role in junk mail rape, simply neglect to renew a subscription to a national magazine. Some six weeks before your subscription is due to expire, you receive an expiration notice, a businesslike and unemotional statement of fact that gives no hint of the psychodrama to come.

Ignore the expiration notice and a few weeks later you will get an envelope marked "THERE'S STILL TIME."

Do nothing.

Next comes the fake mailgram with the first hint of desperation manfully concealed under a fake compliment: "KNOWING HOW BUSY YOU ARE WE HAVE MADE ARRANGEMENTS TO EXTEND YOUR SUBSCRIPTION RENEWAL PERIOD FOR TWO MORE WEEKS BECAUSE WE ARE CONFIDENT YOU STILL WISH TO RECEIVE OUR PUBLICATION."

Do nothing.

Next comes the fake telegram—thin, crinkly, Western Union yellow. It says: "WE'RE WAITING FOR YOU!"

Do nothing.

Once you ignore the fake telegram, the fun really starts. The magazine sends you pathetic gifts: an envelope containing a free stamp, and a peculiar ridge that turns out to be a tiny pencil for marking the *yes* block. Now you've got them on "tender hooks," as Alfalfa Bill Murray used to say. Here it is, the chance you've been waiting for. Your chance to frown in Smile Buttonland, your chance to slug a kid, your chance to park with the gimps, your chance to make Mario Cuomo's father's feet bleed some more.

Let bank tellers be warm and cuddly, let car salesmen give me free balloons, let official greeters hug me, let Ronald Reagan pull a one-eyed Navajo-Gypsy female West

Point cadet out of his pocket and read her aloud. It doesn't matter, because I'm now the biggest little sonofabitch in Purkins Corner and it feels *great*.

Donning my green eyeshade, I sat under a twenty-five watt bulb with all my junk mail spread out before me. All those coupons, RSVPs, check-a-blocks, and pledge cards, waiting to be mailed . . . to somebody or other. What to do?

I cackled, then said:

> "I am not shaped for sportive tricks.
> And therefore, since I cannot prove a lover,
> I am determined to prove a villain
> And hate the idle printers of these days.
> Plots have I laid, signatures dangerous,
> By drunken mismailings, confusion and snafus
> To set Amnesty International and Ira Glasser
> In deadly hate the one against the other.
> And if the *American Spectator* be as true and just
> As I am subtle, false and treacherous,
> This day should *Ms.* be mewed up
> About a questionnaire that says that *F.K.*
> Of *Time*'s heirs the subscriber shall be.
> Dive, thoughts, down to my soul—
> Here *Newsweek* comes."

14

THE STATE
OF THE
FUNNY BONE

Any discussion of the problems of being funny in America will not make sense unless we substitute the word *wit* for *humor*. Humor inspires sympathetic, good-natured laughter and is favored by the "healing power" gang. Wit goes for the jugular, not the jocular, and it's the opposite of football; instead of building character, it tears it down.

It's no accident that *wit* is practically an archaic word in American English. Wit has never played well in America, for reasons not hard to discern.

The first is democracy. Wit is not a democratic form; the two adjectives most often used to modify it are those weapons of Renaissance aristocrats, *rapier* and *stiletto*. Most Americans don't stop and think what these words represent, but they know instinctively that wit is elitist.

History bears them out. The last civilizations to welcome wit were those last outposts of aristocracy, eighteenth-century France and England, homes to the famous conversational salons. Aristocrats are comfortable with wit because they're socially secure. Knowing they could get away with anything simply because they were who they were, Versailles courtiers and Whig peeresses traded bons mots and double entendres without restraint.

Then the guillotine started crashing, the Industrial Revolution started clanking, and wit was drowned out in the clamor of democracy and the rise of the middle class. Both found their natural home in America, where no-holds-barred wit fell victim to the desire for respectability and the restraint demanded by social mobility. Pulling yourself up by your bootstraps is an excellent way to choke; living in dread of saying the wrong thing, American climbers rejected wit and embraced that favorite of the self-made man, the tall tale.

The next blow was struck by our great diversity. A heterogeneous population might be good for the body politic but it's bad for the funny bone. Wit and its handmaidens, satire and parody, require a common ground, an audience of conspirators who are privy to your intentions, and a strong point of view—all of which conflict with that miasmic national squish we call "consensus."

Our unmelted pot has truncated American wit by depriving us of a national comic figure or tic that everyone can identify with. The French have the miser, the Irish have the biddy, the Italians have the jealous husband, the English have Colonel Blimp, but what does America have? Paul Bunyan, Dagwood Bumstead, Babbitt, the cracker-barrel philosopher, the traveling salesman, the Southern senator, the Jewish mother, the Boston brahmin, the Main Line Philadelphian, and the good ole boy—to name just a few.

At first glance it seems like a rich comedic heritage with something for everybody—and it is, which is just the trouble. What is funny to millions of Americans leaves millions of others bemused. We may catch cross-cultural jokes but we don't "feel" them; we know the words but not the tune.

A country in which one man's aberration is another

man's ethos obscures wit's most tempting target. If you can't tell who the eccentrics are, you can't tell who the conventional people are, and if you don't know who the conventional people are, it's impossible to be witty at their expense.

Our great diversity also kills the spontaneity that wit needs. In his 1921 book *American Civilization*, historian Harold Stearns called America "a polyglot boarding-house." We have learned to watch our boardinghouse reach when seated at the national dinner table. We are so afraid of giving offense to this or that group that we have turned into oral basket cases.

Our worst nightmare is that backbone of wit, the generalization. Samuel Johnson could say "If you give a Scot something he'll either break it or drink it," but that sort of remark would cause mass cardiac arrest in the land of the free and the home of Jimmy the Greek. Teddy Kennedy, Jesse Jackson, Daniel Inouye, Gloria Steinem, and Ira Glasser would all go on "Nightline" and say: "*Some* Scots are clumsy drunks, but the vast majority of Scottish-Americans are well-educated and responsible citizens."

There goes your sprightly discourse. It's impossible to talk coherently when compassionate humanitarians keep popping up and saying "*some*."

If you want to see the Some Factor in action, watch Phil Donahue. The show that sticks in my mind featured a white Lesbian, a black Lesbian, and the black Lesbian's child, who had been fathered by the white Lesbian's brother via artificial insemination. The show was already a perfect gift for the feminist who has everything, but Donahue had to add even more democratic balance. When the white Lesbian, who was from Louisiana, said that her mother had "all the prejudices about color that Southerners have," Philippe Egalité leaped in with "*Some* Southerners."

Not daring to trust each other to filter sweeping statements, we clutter up our speech and writing with awkward adverbial easements like "generally speaking" and "by and large," dragging in carefully documented exceptions on the grappling hooks of equivocation until we get so tangled up in what we're trying *not* to say that we produce oxymoronic gems—as when we try to be fair to every ethnic group and come out with "Americans of all nationalities." Hardly what Alexander Pope had in mind when he defined wit as "what oft was thought, but ne'er so well expressed."

Wit is rooted in the personality traits of the intelligent loner. The witty person characteristically takes a dim view of human nature and may even be a misanthrope like Jonathan Swift, who inadvertently gave us a chummy figure of speech when he said "I hate and despise the animal called Man, though I like the occasional Tom, Dick or Harry." That sort of sentiment, like Dorothy Parker's definition of wit—"the humor of the indifferent"—does not go over big in a land where headline writers see nothing wrong with "HEARTS GO OUT TO BRAINLESS BABY."

Our desperate commitment to love 'n' compassion makes us reject corrosive rejoiners in favor of the bland, hale-fellow-well-met heartiness and tense jocularity of the toastmaster's gentle dig. Even on the rare occasions when some American does get savagely indignant, he instinctively reins himself in and tries to blunt his remarks. Asked what should be done about Jerry Falwell, Barry Goldwater flashed a friendly grin and said, "Somebody ought to kick him in the ass." It was supposed to be funny, but as Somerset Maugham observed, "There's not much kick in the milk of human kindness."

Goldwater's retort makes one recall Cyrano's line, "Oh, sir, what you *could* have said," in his speech about the art of insult. Many years ago in a similar exchange, an American produced a witticism that would have won plaudits from both Cyrano and Maugham. Asked what he thought of William Jennings Bryan, the frosty Charles Francis Adams replied, "He is in one sense scripturally formidable, for he is unquestionably armed with the jawbone of an ass." Today such a statement would be a candidate for damage control.

Nice Guyism and melting pot nervousness have made a mortal sin of "putting people down," but the practice has its uses. Certain kinds of unflattering jokes have always helped keep society functioning in a reasonably civilized way.

In the one about the old goat and the spring chicken, pitiless references to the "foolish age" used to discourage many older men from acting out their fantasies lest they end up in a punchline. Now smarmy compassion has joined forces with pseudo-science to produce solemn pronouncements like "self-realization" and "mid-life crisis" that give such men a perfect guiltless excuse to jump the fence.

Bemoaners of sexual harassment might like to recall that the traveling salesman joke protected unescorted women from unwelcome attentions. Known unflatteringly as a "drummer" or a "masher," the anecdotal traveling salesman became such a nationally famous symbol of crudeness that a woman could get rid of an importunate man merely by calling him by the generic name. She may have been less than respectable herself but it didn't matter; a traveling salesman was worse. Theodore Dreiser was able to make the complaisant heroine of *Sister Carrie* a sympathetic character because she was seduced by traveling salesman Charles Drouet. After that, nothing was her fault.

The iceman joke saved bored housewives from themselves. The punchline scene of the husband coming home unexpectedly and finding a block of melting ice on the kitchen floor was so firmly embedded in the national psyche that people dreaded getting involved in a clumsy afternoon amour; the human spirit recoils from the idea of turning into a cliché. Today, however, such a comedy of errors is given the humorless name of "encounter" and credited with saving marriages.

No less a humanitarian than George Orwell defended putting people down when he wrote: "Jokes about nagging wives and tyrannous mothers-in-law . . . do at least imply a stable society in which marriage is indissoluble and family loyalties taken for granted."

Our quest for bigger 'n' better is at odds with wit. Well-aimed thrusts depend upon subtlety, understatement, and a poker face, as in Noel Coward's definition of a gentleman: "A man who can play the bagpipes, but doesn't." But the American mind associates subtlety with sneakiness, understated with underhanded, and poker faces with hostile Indians.

American pragmatism is another of wit's enemies. We want everything to be practical and useful, but the pinnacle of wit is the "jeu d'esprit"—wit for its own sake, with no purpose but sheer joy in words. The jeu d'esprit ought to be popular in a country obsessed with every other kind of game, but it collides with our preference for the quick 'n' easy. It takes a lot of reading and reflection to come up with puns, maxims, epigrams, and ripostes, but Americans can't be bothered. Our wish to be clever without going to the trouble of being learned is reflected throughout our culture. One example is *Cosmopolitan*'s notorious italics, designed to substitute for archness. Another is the pillow talk scene in mass market movies and novels.

Max Ehrlich's *Reincarnation in Venice* encourages people who don't have anything witty to say to say it anyway. Herewith the lovers as they wake up in bed together and have a go at sexual repartee:

> "My dear Mr. Drew."
> "Yes, Miss Knox?"
> "This is to inform you that it has been quite an adventure to have you in my bed. You will do. Speaking as a primitive, as a vital and lusty female,

you will most definitely do, sir. You are what we call a very macho man. Very."

"There happens to be a reason for that."

"Yes?"

"You are a very female female."

She laughed and kissed him for that. "You know, we could stay in bed all day."

"We could."

"Except that would be just too decadent. I mean, even us sybarites have to take time out to eat. Why don't we make a supreme effort? I mean, get out of bed while I make us some breakfast. After that. . . ."

That's the most rollicking bedroom jeu d'esprit since *Atlas Shrugged*.

Wit cannot survive a Noah's Ark atmosphere dominated by self-conscious pairing. Speaking on America's worship of marriage, our leading expatriate Henry James said, "An amiable bachelor here and there doesn't strike me as at all amiss, and I think he too may forward the cause of civilization." Wit flourished in the conversational salons of eighteenth-century Europe largely because these gatherings were not attended by "couples." By contrast, American husbands and wives go everywhere together and spend the evening signaling each other about what *not* to say with daggerish stares, elbows in the ribs, kicks under the table, and hisses of "Shut *up*!" lest a clever riposte arouse fear and loathing in the other married couples who go everywhere together.

These are the same people who reply "a good sense of humor" in surveys about the qualities they look for in a mate. They say it because they know they're supposed to say it; they know they're supposed to say it because they read "Laughter: The Best Medicine" in *Reader's Digest*. What they mean is something quite different. The man

146

who claims to want a wife with a good sense of humor is looking for that quality of benumbed resignation found in women of the type known as "good sports"; the woman who claims to want a husband with a good sense of humor is actually looking for someone who won't be mean to the children.

The most important reason why wit fails in America is sexual insecurity. Wit is aggressive and therefore masculine; at the same time, it's waspish and therefore feminine. Therefore, witty people are queer.

The witty woman is a tragic figure in American life. Wit destroys eroticism and eroticism destroys wit, so women must choose between taking lovers and taking no prisoners.

As with stilettos and rapiers, the name of the game is adjectives. A woman who is *sharp, incisive*, and *surgical* is displeasing to men. Fear of being called a castrating female makes the majority of women rein themselves in and blunt their remarks lest they say to a man, as Dorothy Parker did, "With the crown of thorns I wear, why should I worry about a little prick like you?"

Wit also requires an infinite supply of attitudes that have been bred out, trained out, and knocked out of women for centuries. Taught to say "I love people," "sex is beautiful," and her prayers, the average woman finds it impossible to summon the sang-froid, contempt, impatience, sarcasm, pessimism, blasphemy, and bawdiness required to crack ice at thirty paces.

This state of affairs supposedly changed with the advent of feminism. Throughout the seventies, enormous efforts were made to get women to laugh at previously forbidden topics. Anthologies of humor for women appeared (including one called *Titters* containing a reprint of one of my pieces), but for the most part the silence was deafening. Not that women didn't try. In a letter to *Cosmopolitan* about an article of mine, the reader allowed as how it probably was funny, but concluded with a mixture of plaintiveness and moral superiority: "I guess I take sex seriously."

One problem was the mixed signals feminists gave out. On the one hand they urged women to be raucous and bawdy, while on the other they promoted the *I Am a Humorless Feminist* teeshirt. Another problem was the catch-all nature of the Women's Movement. If, like the Suffragettes, feminists had concentrated exclusively on women and ignored other dispossessed groups, they could have helped women develop the healthy selfishness that lies behind the merry outlook. But in their zeal to stroke and identify with every have-not cause under the sun, they created a chaos of caring that forced women back into the age-old female trap of putting others before self.

The women-and-wit conundrum came to a head in a 1976 book called *The Curse: A Cultural History of Menstruation* by Janice Delaney, Mary Jane Lupton, and Emily Toth. In a chapter on menstruation jokes, this earnest trio came up with one of the finest oxymorons of all time: "We would like to think that feminism will help women develop a different sense of humor, one that is warm, loving, egalitarian, compassionate."

That's like telling people to have calm orgasms.

One of the hardest things for the world to accept is a woman who laughs at sex while remaining above the battle. A woman is never allowed to be detached about sex. She must either pull out all the stops and be filthy—what night-club comics call "working blue"—or make herself the butt of the joke and poke fun at her own sexuality.

I ran up against both of these non-choices in the seventies when I wrote for two new magazines aimed at liberated women. The first was *Playgirl*, whose male publisher conceived the idea of a monthly fictional vignette centering around a funny sexual encounter. The editor asked me to write it and passed on the publisher's instructions: "Make it raunchy."

I have always thought that *raunch* ought to be the French word for "armpit," like *manche* for "sleeve." The difference between raunchy and witty can be illustrated by two remarks on the same subject. The raunchy remark is from a movie whose title I have forgotten. In one scene a couple who work together are about to have sex on an office desk when the phone rings. The man answers it and says, "I can't talk now. Something big has come up."

The witty remark was made by the Edwardian actress Mrs. Patrick Campbell, the first Eliza Doolittle, who eloped during rehearsals of *Pygmalion*. When she returned to work after a four-day honeymoon, George Bernard Shaw asked, "What is this new husband of yours like?" Replied Mrs. Pat: "Six-feet-four and everything in proportion."

I lasted through three *Playgirl* vignettes. The one that got me fired was about a woman who was so desperate to find her clitoris that she decided to use a divining rod. The publisher blew up when he read my lead: "The clitoris is the whistlestop between maidenhead and personhood on the feminist train of thought." The editor told me later that he stormed through the office waving my manuscript and yelling, "That's not raunchy! Suppose Linda Lovelace had said that in *Deep Throat*? It would've ruined the movie!"

Next *Viva*, the sister publication of *Penthouse*, asked me to be their sex advice columnist, a contributing editorship with my name on the masthead. It was the heyday of the kinky sex fad; the readers desperately wanted to believe that earnest cliché, "Anything two people do together is right as long as it doesn't hurt anybody else," so I was

149

under orders to find a funny way of reassuring them that sex is beautiful.

I quickly discovered that when the Penthouse empire tells a woman to be funny, they really mean "kooky." I have always thought that *kook* ought to be the Arabic word for a woman who has a nervous breakdown in the middle of a belly dance. A kook is a sick handmaiden assigned to the male tent and given the job of seeing to it that men always laugh at, never with, the female sex. She accomplishes this by combining Belle Watling's heart of gold with Aunt Pittypat's instability to become the kind of sex partner men call "that crazy kid." A century ago a kook was a girl who jumped naked out of a cake at stag parties; today she's the chief purveyor of the attitude known as "nonjudgmental."

Viva expected me to top the sexual experiences related by the readers with even more bizarre ones—real or imagined—of my own, and to write in a warm and friendly wait-till-I-tell-you-what-I-did tone calculated to soothe their guilty fears and make them feel loved.

Here is the letter that got me fired:

"Q: My boyfriend wants me to stick a lighted Fourth of July sparkler in his ass while we fuck. Is this wrong?

A: No, provided he has more than one ass to give for your country."

150

15   SUPERGOY

It's been eleven years since I published the Wasp book. It was called *Wasp, Where Is Thy Sting?* and everybody thought I was the ideal person to write it. My agent doesn't call me Supergoy for nothing: being the child of an old-line Southern Wasp mother and a British father, I am an enriched version of the breed, as shot full of additives as Wonder Bread.

I decided that being a tenth-generation Wasp on one side and a first-generation English-American on the other would help me infuse the book with the balance needed to make it appealing to Wasps and ethnics alike. The Daughters had landed at Ellis Island and the beachhead was about to be secured.

I was wrong. No Wasp can write a Wasp book because we're the most divided group in America.

I was two pages into the introduction when I ran into the biggest snag. Southerners might be Waspier than anybody else but we are so outré historically and socially that we screw up any book we get into. No book about Wasps can omit Southerners, but no book that includes Southerners can really be a Wasp book.

A writer must write about what he knows, however, so my first draft turned into a sequel to my first book, *Southern*

Ladies and Gentlemen. My editor, a Nebraska Wasp, called me with her evaluation.

"You've left something out," she said tactfully.

Specifically, I had left out everything west of the Mississippi. My editor wanted more on midwestern Wasps, but except for her and the characters in Sinclair Lewis and William Inge, I had never known any. It was more than a lack of physical contact. I had never known any New England Wasps either, but as a Southerner I understand them instinctively because we share a certain ingrown, overbred craziness (there's nothing like being in America for a really long time). I have no trouble identifying with the dark violence and twisted emotions of Lizzie Borden, Ethan Frome, and the characters in *The Scarlet Letter*, but the neurotic propriety of *Splendor in the Grass* leaves me bemused.

My editor cranked me up as much as she could with examples from her own experience, but I was writing through a psychological blind spot. I simply could not plug in to midwestern Wasps. Minor social customs were perplexing enough—do you realize that these people actually eat dinner as soon as it's ready instead of getting half drunk first?—but when I got to religion I was stranded.

I am a Wasp only in the genetic sense; the *P* does not quite apply. As an Episcopalian I am technically an Anglican Catholic, meaning that I have a real feel for theological dottiness untainted by deeper questions of religious belief. I have no religious beliefs to speak of, but I stand four-square with the Highs against the Lows on Latin and incense, and I will go to bat for transubstantiation even though it means nothing to me one way or the other.

I am also drawn to what the Upper South calls "Maryland Catholicism"—an older, landed version of the faith closer to the Stuart crown than to the Knights of Columbus. I don't care whether church and state are separate as long as church and stateliness go hand in glove.

How, then, was I to write about my editor's Methodist childhood? As a Southerner I knew about noisy Protestants, but what can you say about quiet Protestants?

I began to question the strength of our common Englishness. If my problems with Middle America were any guide, it meant nothing. Wasps come in so many different varieties that we're all each other's *them*.

Watch us in Europe and you'll see why we don't "stick together" at home. The Des Moines tourists demanding to know the price of something in "real money" are put off by the members of the Bowdoin College seminar, who are put off by the ancestor-hunting Virginia Daughters, who are put off by the liberated Junior Year Abroad girls, who are put off by the blustering Texas businessmen, who are ready to kill the members of the Bowdoin seminar because they're a bunch of egghead Communist queers.

When all of these groups come together in a sidewalk cafe, they eye one another like the Guelphs and the Ghibellines, bemoan each other's "awful voices," and boast to any native willing to listen that they and they alone are the "*real* Americans. . . . We're not like those terrible people over there at that other table."

Wasp, Where Is Thy Sting? flopped. Part of the trouble was that nobody could find it. Because the title is a pun on *I Corinthians*, some bookstores shelved it under inspirational literature along with suffer-not tracts like *Hey, God, Are You Listening*? Evidently a question mark in a title suggests a spiritual crisis. Other stores shelved it under insects. A few relegated it to the new science of thanatology in the belief that it was a parental guide along the lines of *How To Help Your Child Cope With Death*, and one store stocked it in the juvenile section because they thought it was the story of William the Wasp, born without a stinger, who is mocked and persecuted by his nestmates until he teaches them the meaning of peace and love by becoming the pet of a little crippled boy.

If a Wasp can't write a Wasp book, does it follow that an ethnic can? According to a 1987 book, *The Wasp Mystique* by Dr. Richard C. Robertiello and Diana Hoguet, it's midnight in America and every member of Colonial Banes is a direct descendant of the Evil One.

Psychiatrist Robertiello is in the throes of a negative transference against the people who keep saying "Tennis, anyone?" Contending that America has been enervated by a "misguided idealization and emulation of WASPs," he runs barefoot through all the clichéd Anglo-Saxon traits and taboos and explains how they have ruined the country.

This nasty little book is saved from being infuriating by a literary style that provides comic relief on almost every page.

Wasp Courage: "How often have we heard someone referred to as a real s.o.b.—but he sure has guts. Yes, but guts in the context of what—being an s.o.b., that's what. Blame WASP Mystique for our failure to consider this sufficiently in making our evaluations."

Wasp Good Taste: "It's another example of the degree to which the WASP Mystique has been accepted by our culture. Other cultures clearly have different definitions of 'good' taste—including belching and throwing up, as our anthropologists can attest."

Wasp Emotion: "A definite nay-say for WASPs . . . But being attached to a strong silent man or an ice queen has its deficits. Ask the man who owns one."

Wasp Ambition: "Fighting down this trait is a mixed blessing. It may, in fact, inhibit the ability to maximize potential in whatever arena chosen."

Wasp Hard Work: "It's not enough for its own sake. Besides, 'all work and no play makes Jack a dull boy.' Likewise Jill."

Wasp Families: "Because no matter how much emotional trouble the WASP family is in, they will go on denying it until they are blue in the face. Blue is an intended pun here—blue for blueblood aspired to, for never saying I'm sorry, for being the regal super-cool ruler, even while the royal house is falling down."

American interest in the British royal family upsets Robertiello so much that he loses what little command of syntax he has. Our magazines devoted "reams of ink" to the royal wedding, he charges, and virtually deified the Prince of Wales because "Charles was exemplary of how one should comport himself."

When the stereotyping has run its course, Robertiello backs up his claims with dreary case histories from his patient file ("Myra's story epitomizes the state of the broken WASP") and tosses in a mother who is called "Mumsy."

He saves his most verbose whack for the Wasp stars of the Iran-Contra hearings—Oliver North, John Poindexter, and Fawn Hall. In a final brakeless slide down Bunker Hill that reads like an excerpt from the Choctaw edition of *Psychology Today*, he says that their disregard of the law "has the ring of the supervening superiority of the mystique of the WASP and its claim to a moral ascendancy justifying its preeminence in our society for WASPs and their multitude of pretenders."

I swear by Mario Cuomo's father's bleeding feet that I have copied these passages correctly.

About the only Wasp stereotype that Robertiello missed is the martini. It's just as well he didn't get into it because he would have gone mad. The martini is supposed to be *the* Wasp drink, and it is—except that it isn't. As if to add a final fillip to our schismatic games, the Waspiest region of America has no use for it.

Trying to find a good martini below the Smith & Wesson line is as futile as trying to find a rare steak. Different Southerners have different versions of martiniphobia. To the aging flower of chivalry the martini triggers visions of brittle women. To the crustaceous dowager it threatens that genteel female gathering called a "Saturday Sherry."

To the Baptist it's an Episcopalian plot against iced tea. To the unreconstructed Rebel it's the portent of yet another New South. And to the good ole boy it stands for men who don't like whiskey. Jim Bob and T.J. harbor another objection as well: martinis are drunk out of "little dinky" glasses.

Birmingham: I ordered a martini straight up and they put it in a water goblet. Five inches of glass and half an inch of martini. If you think that saying "half-empty" instead of "half-full" is the sign of a pessimist, try saying "nearly gone" while looking at a martini you haven't even touched.

I complained and the waitress explained.

"We believe in givin' you plenny of room. You know how it is when evrathang's all in there togethuh."

Do Jim Bob and T.J. dunk for olives? I wouldn't put it past them.

Macon: I switched to on-the-rocks. The waitress gave me an approving nod and said: "The iz cuts the bittuh taste. Ah don't see how people can drink 'um 'less they're watered down."

Mine was watered down all right. It was in a champagne glass full of shaved ice—martini sherbet.

Memphis: "Oh, honey, you don't want one of them mean ole thangs. My husband, Alvin, he drunk him some martini once, and lemme tell you, ole Alvin, he just slid right down the wall."

My worst experience occurred when I stopped at a small-town motel while driving through South Carolina. My waitress was a sweet young thing with a big bow in her curly blond hair and a fanned-out lace handkerchief pinned to her shoulder. All in all a classic example of a type the Protestant South produces in droves: the Virgin Mary Lou.

The Virgin Mary Lou's bag has always been simulated innocence. To preserve the girlish purity for which she is famed, she must find something to be completely ignorant about. It used to be sex, but that being impossible to pull off nowadays, she has switched to martinis.

The moment I said "martini" her face crumpled with such despair that she aged six months before my very eyes. She went into the small untended bar and stayed for what seemed like forever. When at last she reappeared, she carried in one hand a cocktail glass containing an olive and about a half inch of liquid. In her other hand was a gin miniature with a peeling label. She sat both down in front of me.

I picked up the miniature and closed my hand around it. It was as warm as the Virgin Mary Lou's smile.

"This is supposed to be cold."

"If you want iz in it, Ah bettuh git you a bigger glass."

"No, this is the right glass, I ordered a martini straight up. I don't want ice *in* it, I just want it cold."

"You mean like a Sebbin 'n' Sebbin?"

"No, a Seven and Seven is a highball. A martini is a cocktail. It's supposed to be mixed with ice."

"Ah kin bring you a l'il bowl of iz if you want."

"No, it's supposed to be *mixed*."

"Ah kin put it in the milkshake machine if you want."

"You can't do that—it would bruise the gin."

"Ma'am?"

"Never mind. What is this greenish stuff in the glass?"

"An olive."

"No, I mean the liquid."

"Oh, that's the othuh part."

"You mean you put the vermouth in the glass first?"

"Ma'am?"

"Vermouth! Do you know what vermouth is?"

"Yes, ma'am, it's up North."

"No. Look. Wait a minute. What did you pour in the glass?"

"A l'il juice from the olive bottle."

"Don't you know how to mix a martini? Didn't they show you?"

"We don't git much call for 'um 'round heah."

"I tell you what. I've changed my mind. I think I'll have a Seven and Seven."

"That's real popular 'round heah," she said with a sweet smile.

Look away, martini lovers.

16

S E X

A N D   T H E

S A X O N   C H U R L

On the first day of school, my junior high English teachers made us write an essay called "What I Did on My Vacation." I always invented healthy, normal activities like sailing and swimming to hide the fact that I had spent the whole two weeks in our beach cottage pantry soaking up Frank Yerby's historical novels.

Thirty years later I wrote a historical novel and ended up in similar circumstances. I turned into a drunk and passed out in the pantry.

By the mid-1970s the anti-feminist backlash had produced a demand for lushly romantic bodice-rippers known in the trade as "sweet savages" after the genre's first blockbuster, *Sweet Savage Love* by Rosemary Rogers. Published as original paperbacks with titles composed of three emotionally extravagant trigger words, they sold into the millions and made their authors rich.

Deciding to get in on the gravy, I contacted a publisher for whom I had done a ghost job.

159

"Great!" he said. "But there's too much Southern plantation and French Revolution. Can you come up with a different background?"

Unfortunately, I could. My first sweet savage mistake was choosing the fall of Roman Britain to the Anglo-Saxons. The fifth century A.D. was the Big Spillover, the Century That Was, when history hit the fan and splattered everywhere. Between the barbarians sacking Rome and the Christians burning down the Hellenic libraries, there was so much destruction that we don't really know what happened, which is why footnotes for the period usually kick off with warnings like "Professor Cholmondeley disagrees."

Like the annexation of Schleswig-Holstein, the fifth century has a way of getting to people who study it. Poor old Cholmondeley was last seen weeping silently in the stacks of the British Museum and grabbing imaginary flies out of the air, but I had to go and choose the fifth century for the sake of freshness.

My editor was delighted, seeing helmets with horns and lots of spiked armor for mauling bosoms in the "he pulled her to him" scenes. I pulled the pen name Laura Buchanan out of a quick brown study and set about creating my heroine. Since she was a British Celt, I gave her red hair and named her Lydda. Her name led to the first of those wacky exchanges that masquerade under the impressive name of "editorial conferences."

"I don't like the name," my editor said. "Too many *d*'s."

"Double-*d* in Welsh is pronounced *th*," I pointed out.

"Yes, but sweet savage readers don't know dat."

I was attached to the name so I persuaded him to keep it, but we got into another wrangle when we tried to come up with a title.

"Something Saxon Splendor," I mused.

"Sweet savage readers don't know what *Saxon* means unless it's got *Anglo* with it, and then you open up another whole can of worms. It'll sound like an ethnic-awareness book. Besides, hyphens scare them."

"Because of ethnic sensitivity?"

"No, because hyphens in titles are scary. They remind them of feminists who keep their maiden names after they get married. We're talking about nervous, frustrated, lonely women here, that's why they read this schlock. If we use *Saxon* we've got to do it in a way that won't make them feel insecure."

"How about Sex and the Saxon Churl?"

"They don't know what *churl* means."

We were stuck in the Something Saxon Splendor groove until my editor decided to abandon the troika mode entirely and go for the romantic fantasy jackpot with a "princess" title.

"The Barbarian Princess," he said proudly.

"They don't know the historical meaning of barbarian," I protested. "They'll think it's about a girl with awful table manners. How about The Celtic Princess?"

"They don't know what *Celtic* means either, but it would remind them of basketball, and that would remind them of their husbands sitting in front of the tube instead of carrying them into the bedroom. We're talking about love-starved women here. Don't worry about the historical meaning. Barbarian sounds sexy."

We called the book *The Barbarian Princess* and I began constructing a plot. I use the word loosely because not even Aristotle could get a plot out of the fifth century. Besides, I didn't really need one. A plot is a mathematically balanced and logically structured series of events leading to the resolution of a conflict. The genre I was in called for that incorrect but widespread definition of a plot known as "a lot happens." In keeping with the typical sweet savage, mine was a sadomasochistic daisy chain of incidents based on the popular wisdom of the hour: "When in doubt, rape."

My editor counseled me carefully on the need to strike the proper balance between erotic titillation and romantic idealism. He was worried about me, and with good reason. So far my "real" books under my own name had been nonfiction, and I was known as a humorist—always fatal to romance. We're talking about women who take sex seriously here. Worse, I had been a pornographer; between 1968 and 1972 I wrote thirty-seven paperback porn novels in which I was supposed to sound like a man and did.

"Remember," he cautioned, "keep the heroine a virgin as long as possible, and never let her have sex *willingly* with a man she doesn't love."

I began in a mood of enthusiasm that was not entirely mercenary. I love history and wanted to be factually correct, to give the book an authentic period flavor. Since Roman Britons spoke Latin, I decided to toss in a few obvious phrases for the sake of verisimilitude.

The story opens in the early spring of 409 with Lydda swimming naked in the Bristol Channel, so when she entered the water I had her exclaim *"Quam frigida est!"* Chased by a boatful of Roman sailors patrolling for Saxon and Hibernian pirates, she cries *"Desiste!"* when one of them jumps into the water and grabs her. Later, unable to find her mirror while dressing for dinner, she asks her maid, *"Ubi speculum est?"*

My editor called me as soon as he read it.

"Go easy on the Latin. Sweet savage readers can't handle all that. You can have her scream *desiste* when she gets raped, though."

Since time and place were right, I gave Lydda a childhood sweetheart named Patricius who tells her about a strange dream he had about wandering through the neighboring island of Hibernia fighting off snakes. It brought a delighted phone call from my editor.

"I told Publicity we're going to be first on the market with the seduction of Saint Patrick!"

I devised a better idea that would save Lydda's virginity and allow me to dramatize a factual incident. She and Patricius go for a chariot ride and end up necking in a field. Just as he is about to "take" her, Hibernian pirates burst out of the woods, throw nets over them, and drag them back to the ship to sell them as slaves in the snake-infested Auld Sod. (This is how Ireland ended up with a Brit for her patron saint).

Screaming "*desiste!*" Lydda is taken to the captain's quarters, but just as he is about to rape her, she kicks him in the *globuli* and jumps overboard. Since I set her up as a strong swimmer in the first chapter, she makes it back to Britannia, where more trouble bodes. As soon as she recovers from her ordeal, her father announces that he has chosen a husband for her: the evil and corrupt Roman, Vitellinus, whom she hates.

In Londinium for her wedding, Lydda meets the Saxon general Thel, a blond hunk in spiked armor who has come to negotiate a peaceful colonization plan with the Roman Britons to save him the trouble of conquering their country.

It's love-hate at first sight. Thel pulls Lydda to him the first chance he gets. "*Desiste!*" she cries, as well she might, because by the time I got through with his armor it looked like Kaiser Bill's helmet.

On their wedding night, Vitellinus doesn't notice the shredded condition of her bosom because he has no interest in her front. Just to keep her virginity perking along, I made him a sodomist who forces her to submit to beastly practices that leave her hymen intact.

They go to Rome where Lydda meets the emperor's promiscuous sister, Placidia, whose hobby is destroying innocence. She offers Lydda her own newest lover, a Saxon general of immense talents (here I borrowed Mrs. Patrick Campbell's famous assessment, "Six-feet-four and everything in proportion") who has recently arrived in Rome.

None other than Thel the Hunk. It's *desiste* time again, but since Lydda loves-hates him, she lets him ravish her. Not long after their passionate interlude, she is conveniently widowed when the psychotic Vitellinus commits suicide. Now she and Thel are free to marry and live happily ever after, but I was only on page two hundred. The lovers had to be separated somehow so Lydda could live to scream "*desiste!*" some more.

History came to my rescue. By now it was August of 410, so I sent Thel out of town on a government mission and left Lydda alone in Rome so she could be kidnapped by Alaric the Goth when he swings through on his sack.

Somewhere around this time I started to drink. I had always liked a little snort but now I began downing bourbon in the classic Southern manner. No matter how much pride I took in my research, no matter how much Latin I added for flavor, the fact remained that I was spinning a pointless, plotless, endless chase scene whose only purpose was keeping a good-bad girl one step ahead of the long short-arm of the lawless.

Since Alaric the Goth died of a stroke three weeks after the sack of Rome, I made it happen while he was raping Lydda. Fleeing from his tent, she steals a horse and gallops off to find Thel, but she is waylaid by an evil Egyptian sea captain who kidnaps her to Alexandria and delivers her to the sexually insatiable Roman prefect, Orestes, for whom he pimps. Orestes installs her in his luxurious palace and she becomes, against her will, a bird in a gilded cage.

In Alexandria, Lydda makes friends with the famous female scholar Hypatia. The association between the city's most notorious courtesan and its most liberated career woman provokes the ire of Archbishop Cyril, Alexandria's misogynistic prelate, who sends a band of monks to murder them. As Lydda watches in horror, the monks cut Hypatia to pieces with oyster shells (true) and then come after her.

Leaping into a tradesman's parked wagon, she flees into

the desert where she is taken hostage by a pair of early Christian hermits busily mortifying their flesh. To prove their immunity to female charms, they strip her naked and force her to lie in bed between them while they pray.

Just as she is about to be beaten for causing an erection, Roman troops arrive and torch the hermit colony. Fleeing from the burning hut without a stitch on, Lydda is arrested by Lucius the Centurion, who takes his pleasure with her and then turns her over to his men. Screaming "*desistite!*" (gang rape takes the plural), she proves such a delectable spitfire that Lucius decides to sell her to the keeper of Constantinople's most select brothel.

There she meets Marcellus the Eunuch, who becomes her friend (my editor called this her "free time"). Together they concoct a plan to escape from their mutual captivity and stow away on a ship bound for Britannia.

By now I was drinking one day, sobering up the next, and writing on the third, which explains what happens next. During a storm at sea, a falling mast crushes Marcellus, and the captain and the entire crew are washed overboard, leaving Lydda alone on a rudderless ship.

Weak from hunger, she faints just as the ship founders on a craggy rock. She comes to in the arms of a craggy man in black robes.

"Where am I?" she asks.

"Caledonia."

"Who are you?"

"Nagar the Druid."

That was the day I passed out in the pantry.

Of course Nagar ravishes her—it's the only way sweet savage characters can get a conversation going. He does it on a stone altar in the sacred oak grove, injecting her with so much Celtic awareness that she becomes a Druid priestess and leads an army of wild Caledonians into Britannia to wrest her homeland from the Saxon churls.

Borne on her chariot, her face painted blue, she charges the leader of the hated Sassenach, but lo and behold. . . .

Reunited with Thel the Hunk on the battlefield, she is routed, raped, and married in short order. The wedding ceremony is performed by Patricius, home on leave from a now snake-free Hibernia, and nine months later he baptizes their son.

By now I weighed one hundred and eighty pounds and had a twitching eyelid. The hectic mess I had written sold for such a large sum that my editor asked me to write another one, this time using a background of ancient Greece. The title search began all over again.

"How about *Something Golden Glory*?" he said.

"How about *Chaos and Meander*?"

"Too mythy."

That did it. Another round of this would kill me.

"It's time to cease and *desiste*," I said.

17

PHALLUS
IN
WONDERLAND

Mel Berger
William Morris Agency
1350 Avenue of the Americas
New York, New York 10019

Dear Mel:

I got a call from a lady at *Lear's* magazine who
asked me if I could do a critique of John Updike's
novels. I said yes, but we've got a problem. Remember when a reporter asked Gerald Ford what
he thought of Solzhenitsyn and Ford said, "I understand he's superb"?

I've never read John Updike. Naturally I didn't
tell the *Lear's* lady that, so when you call her to
negotiate the nuts and bolts, please invent some
reason to ask for a long deadline so I'll have time
to read the major novels.

Florence

Florence King
1861 Robert E. Lee St.
Fredericksburg, Virginia 22401

Dear Florence:

It's all set. I told the *Lear's* lady you needed some time "to refresh your memory" so you've got two months. I understand Updike is a genius. Read him in good health.

Mel

Dear Mel:

I've started *Poorhouse Fair*. Updike's style is an exquisite blend of Melville and Austen: reading him is like cutting through whale blubber with embroidery scissors.

Here's the sunrise: "Despite the low orange sun, still wet from its dawning, crescents of mist like the webs of tent caterpillars adhered in the crotches of the hills."

Here's the sunset: "Opaque air had descended to the horizon, hills beyond the housetops of the town. On one side, the northern, a slab of blue-black, the mantle of purple altered, reared upward; on the other inky rivers tinged with pink fled in one diagonal direction. Between these two masses glowed a long throat, a gap flooded with a lucent yellow whiter than gold, that seemed to mark the place where, trailing blue clouds, a sublime creature had plunged to death. . . ."

It goes on like that for a whole page. Somebody also has "wine-dark lips." Isn't that from *The Odyssey*?

He was awfully young when he wrote *Poorhouse Fair* so I'm going to skip it and start *Rabbit, Run*.

I'm sure I'll like it better—the critic Milton Rugoff once said it had "all the force and brilliance of a hallucination."

Florence

Dear Mel:

It does. Listen to this: "They pelted the soldiers with remarks like balls of dust and the men sneezed into laughter." That's the kind of sentence that makes Magic Markers the biggest-selling item in undergraduate bookstores—it saves writing "How true!" in the margins.

Rabbit, Run is about a sensitive, tormented basketball star who runs away from his wife—a *belles-lettres* version of *Hoosiers* with an undescended testicle. Rabbit is searching for "something that wants him to find it." He spends a lot of time wandering around trying to decide what it is he's searching for. To discover the object of Rabbit's quest, I consulted one of those slim lit. crit. monographs that English professors like to write. This is what the author, Rachael Burchard, said:

> *The author seems to be telling us that "the search is the thing," that instinct or intuition demands that we search. Or perhaps he is saying that anyone, whether he be intellectual or faithful or immoral and simple can sense the reality of God. Perhaps he is saying that God tries to reach us.*

Florence

Dear Florence:

Keep them searches and seizures coming.

Mel

Dear Mel:

I gave up on Rabbit and started on *The Centaur*. It opens with a high school teacher named George Caldwell being shot in the ankle with an arrow in the middle of a lecture on the solar system. As he leaves the classroom in search of first aid, he turns into Chiron the Centaur.

The novel is an allegory based on ancient Greek mythology—except when it isn't.

Turning back into a man, Caldwell goes to Hummel's Auto Body Shop to get his ankle treated.

You heard me: He goes to a mechanic to get the arrow removed from his ankle. Why? Because he has trusted mechanics ever since one told him his car was a heap. He received the news with joy, saying, "You've told me what you think is the truth and that's the greatest favor one man can do for another."

I consulted the lit. crit. monograph again. Here's what author Burchard wrote:

> The Centaur *appears to be a part of Updike's search for new dimensions in religion which will satisfy the needs of the neoteric individual. As in much of the poetry and in* Rabbit, Run, *it stresses the confusion of our time, especially for the dedicated seeker after Truth.*

So, being a dedicated seeker after Truth, Caldwell gets Honest Hummel to yank the arrow. Afterwards he returns to school. As he passes the girls' gym he sees Hummel's wife, Vera, who teaches phys. ed., standing naked in the dressing room, "her amber pudenda whitened by drops of dew."

Says she: "Why should my brother Chiron stand gaping like a satyr? The gods are not strange to him." The allegory is on again; Caldwell has turned back into a centaur and Vera has become Venus. She continues: "Father Kronos, in the shape of a horse, sired you upon Philyra in the fullness of his health; whereas at my begetting he tossed the severed genitals of Uranus like garbage into the foam."

After she propositions him ("Come, Chiron, crack my maidenhead, it hampers my walking"), the centaur turns back into Caldwell and returns to his classroom, where the kids throw BBs at him. Three days later, Caldwell-Chiron dies and becomes a constellation right up there with Uranus. The book ends with a quotation in classical Greek.

To find out what it all meant, I consulted another lit. crit. monograph. This is what Joyce Markle said: *"Thus, the overt use of myth in this manner allows Updike to control the extent and direction of his ambiguity."*

Isn't "controlled ambiguity" like "Lebanese government" or "Mexican economy"? I don't know how much more of this I can stand.

Florence

Dear Florence:

Last night at a literary cocktail party I met an Updike scholar who has a theory you might find useful. He said: "Unlike Hemingway and Mailer, Updike doesn't transpose the military experience to the monads of his imaginary cosmos."

I didn't ask him what it meant because I was afraid he might tell me, but it has something to do with the fact that Updike was never in the service. I hope this will inspire you.

Mel

Dear Mel:

All right, you parseheads, I wanna see some
sensitivity around here. You came here to Camp
Jejune as full-blooded readers, but we're gonna
turn you into Sublimes!

I got somethin' here I want you plot-suckin' de-
nouements to listen to. It's from General John
"Chesty" Updike's novel *A Month of Sundays*: "Dear
Tillich, that great amorous jellyfish, whose faith was
a recession of beyonds with these two flecks in one
or another pane: a sense of the world as 'theon-
omous,' and a sense of something 'unconditional'
within the mind. Kant's saving ledge pared finer
than a fingernail."

That oughta show you pudendas what happens
when the Sublimes waft ashore and hit the imaginary cosmos. Chesty Updike refracts hell out of
those monads and secures Fragmentary Hill
quicker than you can say trompe l'oeil. That's why
the Sublime motto is Semper Vortex! Now get ur-
anuses over to the monograph range on the double!

Florence

Dear Florence:

While thumbing through my Articles Due file,
your *Lear's* card reared up before me. In the suddenly opaque air a mantle of fear descended upon
me, dappling my flanks with rivulets of sweat as I
saw that Time's wingèd Chevy is running out on
the Updike piece.

Mel

Dear Mel:
Call me Ishkabibble.
I'm now reading *Couples*. It's about ten couples

in a suburb named Tarbox and they're all searching. Twenty—count 'em—*twenty* dedicated seekers after Truth, saying things like "Maybe he is because I am, because we are" and "Death excites me. Death is being screwed by God."

The theme is sex 'n' death: the thinking man's jiggly. The protagonist is named Piet, which is Dutch for Pete. His problem, according to lit. crit. author Burchard, is his inability to separate *agape* from passion. He ought to watch Julia Child—she can do it with one hand.

Florence

Dear Florence:

The *Lear's* lady called. She wants to know if you think deadlines are an illusion of reality.

Mel

Dear Mel:

I'm sorry to be so slow but I've been reading *Rabbit Is Rich* and all those references to damp-dark-dank secret places between women's thighs got to me. I have come down with a mysterious bladder infection. The doctor said it's *tant pis*.

I've also been busy around the house. Having read detailed descriptions of approximately six bushels of pubic hair, nameless forces drove me to go seeking and questing through my kitchen drawer to gather up all the Twisties I've saved and arrange them by color.

I found myself haunted by inexorable visions of all the motes, fragments, mists, films, filigrees, and blackish embryos of cumulus I've been reading about, so I cleaned and scrubbed like a Dutch goodwife. I even covered toothpicks with gauze to get the dirt out of those narrow places between Scylla and Charybdis. It took me four days, but now you could eat off my floor. My apartment is a shining city on a hill and I am a potted plant.

Can't you imagine what Updike could do with Elvis Memorial Day? "The long underbelly of the line reared up with deathly life and a silt of caring fell from worshipper to worshipper as they filtered past the crotch-high statue of a hound dog made of roses. Teenage girls holding soaked yearning between their thighs turn the incipient blisters of their pouty lips toward the crypt as the air fills with the smell of between-breasts gummy with cheap powder. . . ."

Florence

Dear Florence:

The *Lear's* lady called again. Can't you please write something, anything? I persuaded her to extend the deadline for two weeks. Can you manage something of intrinsic significance? Please advise.

Dear Mel:

BERGER, BUT
BY FLORENCE KING

Berger stared at the bruise and dung colors of his office. Voices mossy-thick as a tree where it comes out of the grass scrabbled at him through a hollow blur. There was a boom box stuck on his shoulder. Some street kid had thrown it at him, and now it was embedded in his flesh, locked forever on a hard rock station, turning him into a dedicated seeker after truth who couldn't hear himself seek.

He opened the drawer of his crotch-high file cabinet. The hang files on their tracks reminded him of claws on the guard-rails of transcendence suspended over a primordial pit. Withdrawing a letter, he took it to Father Xerox and pressed the print button. The technological monster transluced into life with a chuffling sound of dolorous vigor like children rollerskating in hell.

The events of Berger's life arranged themselves gummily in his mind like the shoe polish caught in the drilled eyes of his wingtips. He saw himself as a baby, lying in his scabrous crib and playing with his toy contract while Flatus, that great bubbler, sent resounding fanfaronades into the damp, dark, dank depths of his diaper.

He was Berger, but he was someone else.

Suddenly he knows. His stomach slides and a wave of certainty scoops at his chest. He was Bergerion, condemned by Zeus to balance a lyre on his shoulder until Venus got her maidenhead back.

He was a prisoner in the thin-stretched shadows of earthly wilderness now, but someday he would be a constellation in the sky, right up there next to Your Anus.

Florence

Dear Florence:

The *Lear's* lady said she knows exactly what she's seeking after: your Updike piece. Please advise.

Mel

Dear Mel:

When Samuel Johnson was asked to comment on the plot of *Cymbeline* he refused, saying, "It is impossible to criticize unresisting imbecility."

I am at brain-death's door. I can't finish any of Updike's books. I keep putting one down and going on to another, thinking it'll be better, but it never is. His last one, *Roger's Version*, is about a divinity professor and a computer expert who team up to prove the existence of God. Part of it is written in computerese and part in medieval Latin. The lit. crit. crowd called it "a novel of ideas." How can they tell?

For the past month I've been hoping that *Lear's* would self-destruct so I wouldn't have to read John Updike. Last week while deep-frying softshell crabs I got the oil too hot and the pan ignited. It was a Freudian slip—I was trying to burn the house down so I wouldn't have to read John Updike.

I'd rather be a human mine sweeper in the Strait of Hormuz than read John Updike. I'd rather run away and join the ladies auxiliary of the French Foreign Legion than read John Updike. Tell the *Lear's* lady I'm dead—it's more or less true. I've been throwing up, grinding my teeth, and twisting a strand of hair like Olivia de Havilland in *The Snake Pit*.

Florence

Dear Florence:

I've tried to call you several times but there was no answer. I've persuaded the *Lear's* lady to accept a substitute for the Updike piece. Do you happen to have something suitable in the primordial depths of your screeching hang files? Please advise.

Mel

Mel Berger
William Morris Agency
1350 Avenue of the Americas
New York, New York 10019

Dear Mr. Berger:

You don't know me, but I'm Florence King's neighbor here in Virginia.

Now don't you worry, everything's all right. The good news is that Florence will be back home real soon. There's nothing wrong with her mind, she was just a little run down.

The bad news is that she doesn't have a "piece" (I don't know what that means but she said you would), so while we were waiting for the men to come, she asked me to tell you to "send the *Lear's* lady the letters." I don't know what that means either. I don't know what any of this is all about, except that it has something to do with dikes. That's not my cup of tea, but live and let live, I always say.

If you're ever down this way, come see me.

> Yours sincerely,
> Mary Lou Carmichael Monroe
> (Mrs. Stuart Madison Monroe III)

18

WOMEN'S LITTER

Once upon a time, female tractability melded exquisitely with the rules of literary structure to produce some of the most controlled prose in the English language.

Captives of that old devil "niceness," women writers of the past paid close attention to critical admonitions because they sounded so much like the maxims of ladylike behavior that governed their lives. Horace's *"Remember always never to bring/a tame in union with a savage thing"* means don't include a love theme in your murder mystery; but to the well-reared Victorian girl it also meant "Take a chaperon with you."

Boileau's *"Polish, repolish, every color lay/sometimes add, but oftener take away"* means cut, cut, cut until there's not one unnecessary word left; but when woman's place was in the home, it also suggested compliments like "You could eat off her floor."

The result of this happy alliance was the goodwife sentence; a model of order and restraint, with every word subjected to the literary housekeeper's acid test: "You could eat off her manuscript." Classicism joined forces with

the etiquette book and the scrub bucket to give us the shining rigor of *Ethan Frome.*

It's all over now. Free at last to write "like women," today's goodwives are doing just that. In the last fifteen years or so, the woman's novel has turned into the Amtrak of American literature; crashing through the gates at Aristotle, jumping the tracks at Horace, ignoring the flashing red lights at Boileau, and scooping up Alexander Pope in the cowcatcher. The rules are down and it's every stylist for herself in this best of all Tupperware parties, where plot and characterization have been replaced by the kind of non-stop chatter that enabled the French Foreign Legion to meet its enlistment quota for a hundred and fifty years. In the unlikely event that future scholars will bother to give our era a cultural tag, it will be called the Age of Women's Litter.

Everything that goes into a novel should advance either the plot or the characterization. Ruth Harris's 1970 novel *Decades* contains a glaring example of an extraneous passage:

> She bought French bikinis, chic terry beach robes, jeans for deep-sea fishing and white pants for free-port shopping, forty-dollar cotton tops to go with the pants, long dresses of voile for dinner and dancing and cashmere sweaters (they had been revived from the fifties) to throw over them. She bought new underwear and new nightgowns, sneakers and thong sandals (revived from the forties) for evening. She bought new luggage at T. Anthony, had her legs waxed at Arden's and her hair put into condition at Don Lee's. She ordered new makeup in darker shades to go with her suntan, après-sun moisturizing lotion and a portable hair dryer that worked on American and European current.

This is not creative writing, it's a checklist for That Cosmo Girl and it belongs in an article called "What to Pack for Vacation."

A much longer description of clothes appears in *Gone With the Wind* but it bows to Henry James's dictum, "Dramatize, dramatize," by advancing both plot and characterization through its subtle infusion of tension. Because the reader has not yet met Melanie, this passage holds our interest:

> What dress would best set off her charms and make her most irresistible to Ashley? . . . . The rose organdie with the long pink sash was becoming, but she had worn it last summer when Melanie visited Twelve Oaks and she'd be sure to remember it. And might be catty enough to mention it. The black bombazine . . . made her look a trifle elderly. . . . It would never do to appear sedate and elderly before Melanie's sweet youthfulness. The lavender-barred muslin . . . made her look like a schoolgirl. It would never do to appear schoolgirlish beside Melanie's poised self. The green plaid taffeta was her favorite dress. . . . But there was unmistakably a grease spot on the basque. Of course, her brooch could be pinned over the spot, but perhaps Melanie had sharp eyes.

Another favorite area for pointless inventory is home decor. Alice Adams does it in *Superior Women* (1984).

> They all live on the upper East Side; their rooms all are filled with family antiques, plus a few bold "contemporary" touches, here a Noguchi lamp, there an Eames chair. And everywhere a similar weight of wedding presents, the silver or crystal ashtrays, Paul Revere bowls, pewter cocktail shak-

ers. . . . Hers is the most truly elegant apartment of them all; the graceful effect of her (real) Louis Seize chairs is not marred by anything clumsy, Jacobean. And she and Potter are the only couple to have a Robsjohn-Gibbings dining room table.

We learn nothing about Adam's characters from their furniture. By contrast, Nancy Hale's 1942 novel *The Prodigal Women* turns a description of a young society couple's first apartment into a breathtaking description of a frigid woman:

> It showed that the novels were wrong; that commonsense was right; that happy marriages were not made from great love. Great love, on the contrary, could not possibly be fitted into such a chic apartment as this; it would knock over all the little tables.

No longer chained to the stove but feeling perhaps that they ought to be, ostensibly liberated women novelists chain themselves to their typewriters and compose endless grocery lists without purpose as if they were in the grip of a guilty compulsion to fill up a page as women once filled up the stomachs of their loved ones: with food.

The cover price of *The Women's Room* could have been reduced if only somebody had cleared the table. After their first four-legged frolic, Mira and Ben raid the icebox and put together:

> . . . a feast of Jewish salami and feta cheese and hard-boiled eggs and tomatoes and black bread and sweet butter and half-sour pickles and big black Greek olives and raw Spanish onions and beer, and trotted all of it back to bed with them and sat there gorging. . . .

We know what magazine would excerpt this and call it "Sexy Foods to Eat in Bed." The sensual allusions conveyed by the eating scene in the movie *Tom Jones* do not work in print, but a few pages later Mira and Ben have at it again, this time with commas on the side:

> They had guacamole, and Szechuan shrimp, and vegetable curries, and Greek lamb with artichokes and egg lemon sauce; they tried a variety of pastas, bab ganoush, hot and sour soup, sauerbraten, quiche, rabbit stew, and one special night, suprêmes de volaille avec champignons.

At least French keeps her listmaking well within the gourmet range. In *Smart Women* Judy Blume takes us to a fast food joint and force-feeds us one of the dreariest paragraphs ever penned:

> Stuart ate a whole pizza by himself, with pepperoni and extra cheese. Margo, Michelle and Sara shared a large vegie supreme with whole wheat crust. Sara picked the onions and mushrooms off her slice and Michelle picked off the olives. Margo said, "Maybe vegie supreme was the wrong choice."

Food has its uses to writers who understand the principles of a balanced literary diet. In her 1941 murder mystery *Laura*, Vera Caspary used it to characterize one of the hardest types to pin down in print: the heterosexual but overcivilized epicene male known in the South as "an old maid in britches."

> Waldo Lydecker had to have his plate arranged just so, pork on this side, duck over there, noodles under the chicken-almond, sweet and pungent spareribs next to the lobster, Chinese ravioli on a

separate plate because there might be a conflict in sauces. Until he had tried each dish with and without beetle juice, there was no more talk at our table. . . . He snapped his fingers. Two waiters came running. It seems they had forgotten the fried rice. There was more talk than necessary, and he had to rearrange his plate. Between giving orders to the Chinese and moaning because the ritual (his word) of his dinner was upset, he talked about well-known murder cases.

This is known as "foreshadowing," a writer's way of hinting about something to come. Waldo Lydecker was as fastidious about Laura as he was about his food. Unable to bear the thought of her pristine perfection subjected to the runny messes of the marital bed, he decided to murder her on the weekend before her wedding.

A firm editor can send clothes and furniture to the Good Will and clear the table with a slash of the blue pencil. A harder litter to deal with is the ground-in kind caused by lazy evocation of the past.

The Our Song syndrome is a quick 'n' easy way to summon an earlier time. A notorious devotee of this dodge is Ann Beattie, whose *Love Always* opens with Barbra Streisand singing her threnodic version of "Happy Days" and proceeds to grow into an Ascapian mountain range of ditties.

Sara Davidson's needle gets stuck in the same groove in *Friends of the Opposite Sex*. The first chapter, only seven pages long, contains six song titles from the sixties, and an argument between naked lovers over whether "Goodbye, Ruby Tuesday" was on an album called *Between the Buttons*. The lovers get so excited during this passionate wrangle that they get out of bed and comb through the record cabinet in the middle of the night.

No matter where Davidson's characters are or what they

are doing, it always reminds them of a favorite song from their counterculture heyday. A cue arm hangs over their heads like the sword of Damocles. One expresses intense happiness with "I feel like I'm on the cover of an Eagles album, *Hotel California*." The most unseemly plug of all comes when the heroine climbs a mountain in the Sinai and Davidson describes the deep feelings of a Diaspora Jew on first seeing the Promised Land: "A Jimmy Cliff song ran through her head: 'I Want To Know.'"

Songs have literary work to do, and if they don't do it they have no place in a novel. Suspense author Patricia Highsmith got enormous mileage out of a Gay Nineties lyric in her 1950 thriller *Strangers On a Train*. As the evil Bruno stalks through an amusement park, a calliope plays "Casey Would Waltz With the Strawberry Blond." Highsmith very cleverly quoted the line *"Her brain was so loaded it nearly exploded"* because Bruno is planning to strangle Guy's wife. A classic example of the literary technique known as "indirection"—describing something hideous by alluding to something innocent and pleasant—it raises the tension to an unbearable pitch.

Another example of lazy evocation is the Bijou syndrome. Sara Davidson lets one of her characters recite the entire plot of *Picnic* so that we might look into the heart of a disillusioned woman remembering the days when she believed in true love.

In *The Women's Room*, Marilyn French made obsessive use of *Stella Dallas* to drive home the point—gratuitous considering the ongoing story—that women suffer:

> Oh, God! I'll never forget that last scene, when the daughter is being married inside the big house with the high iron fence around it and she's standing out there—I can't even remember who it was, I saw it when I was still a girl, and I may not even be remembering it right. But I am remembering it—

it-it made a tremendous impression on me—anyway, maybe it was Barbara Stanwyck.

Besides being an inadequate way of bringing past emotions and impressions to life, letting characters describe
old movies leads a writer into bad dialogue. Because people
in real life tend to grope for names of stars and directors,
the Bijou syndrome writer has her characters do the same,
ending up with staccato sentences like: "Oh, who—wait . . .
was it . . . yes, it was Paulette what's-her-name . . . you
know, she was married to Charlie Chaplin."

Women's Litter is full of such fits-and-starts dialogue.
Alice Adams is a devotee of the trenchant grunt:

> "Shall we, uh, share a cab?"
> "It's, uh, really spring now."
> "Country smells are, uh, really terrific."
> "I'm, uh, a friend of Janet's."

This sound is not the personal idiosyncrasy of any one
character in *Superior Women*; they all do it, as does the
author in her exposition: "She has never touched him
there, touched his, uh, thing."

Designed to serve verisimilitude—this is the way people
really talk—this sort of writing grates on the reader's
nerves and violates Aristotle's dictum that art must imitate,
never copy, life. People *do* talk this way, but when they do
it in novels it becomes the stylistic offense known as "second
thoughts."

Evoking the past does not require the genius of an
Emily Brontë. All it takes is an awareness of something
called the "brushstroke technique." Edna Ferber, no literary titan but ever the professional, used it in *So Big* when
she covered twelve years of Selena De Jong's life on a
hardscrabble farm with a one-sentence description of her
hairpins: "She skewered her braid with a hairpin from

which the varnish had long since faded, leaving it a dull gray."

It's undemocratic to say anything good about censorship, but why stop now?

Censorship makes writers try harder. In 1911 Edith Wharton could not write a cunnilingus scene, so she had Ethan Frome kiss Mattie's knitting wool instead. The exquisitely subtle passage she turned out is enough to knock your socks off.

Being able to write explicitly about sex has made authors relax and grow careless in other areas of writing, from plotting and pacing to grammar and punctuation. Men do it, too, but the worst offenders are Women's Litters intent upon proving how liberated they are. Exhausted from writing monumentally detailed sex scenes, they give everything else a lick and a promise.

When they have trouble making the story move, they fake action from behind a steering wheel to trick the reader into thinking that someone or something is going somewhere. In *Smart Women*, Judy Blume's heroine "drove up to Fourth, left on Pearl, right on Sixth, across Arapahoe, up the hill to Euclid, right on Aurora to the dead end sign." Also where the reader ends up.

Erica Jong's *Parachutes & Kisses* sounds like a script for "Hardcastle and McCormick." When not in bed, the lubricious Isadora Wing is in her silver Mercedes. She jumps toll booths on the Merritt Parkway, misses freeway exits while stoned, rushes her daughter to the hospital and her dog to the vet, rolls down an icy driveway, crashes into a stone wall—anything to convince the reader that the author is capable of producing some other forward movement besides a pelvic thrust.

Women's Litter abounds with sloppy metaphors and ill-considered descriptions. Judy Blume calls our attention to "a battered Datsun pickup the color of infant diarrhea." Sara Davidson gives us an unintentionally hilarious coupling:

> She could feel the climax now, swishing its tail like a fish. He was pulling it up and out of her. Up and up it came, big, this fish was going to set records, they were going to weigh it, they would pose beside it for photographs. You could see its powerful form rising up through the water, navy blue.

This exquisite metaphor for passion's culmination gets an even more memorable grace note when Davidson plunges in and describes love's afterglow: "They lay spent, slumped together like two wet fish in a bucket."

The increasingly difficult task of coming up with new and different ways to describe the same old sex act gets writers into the habit of straining for everything. Erica Jong tells us that "dawn dyed the Connecticut hills the color of fuchsined water in some recollected apothecary jar." But the book more in need of a truss than a dust jacket is Diana Davenport's *Wild Spenders*:

"She gave him a smile like gin splashed on hot coals."
"Kate's jaw hardened as if her inlays had just fused."
"Bruce whinnied loud, reminding them he was still there, blood Rorschaching around him."
". . . her mound shook and shimmied like a small mad dog."
". . . mascara drooping from her lids like ant doody."

Can it get worse? Yes, because Davenport tries to pun in Latin: "She cruised Will's bookstore until he closed, and carped the diem by going home to make love." This proves that Davenport has had some sort of tenuous encounter with Horace because *carpe diem,* meaning "seize the day," is from his poem "Carmina." The only trouble is, the Cosmo girls who can be counted on to devour Davenport's novel will have no idea what she's talking about. It's ironic that she should have chosen this particular Horatian phrase to have fun with because the line preceding it in the poem is an apt description of how I felt while reading her book: *"Dum loquimur, fugerit invida"* ("While we are speaking, envious time will have flown").

In the area of offenses against grammar and punctuation, Judy Blume gives us "Buck's" County, Pennsylvania; he "hung" himself; and she "spit" out toothpaste. These errors occur not in dialogue where an ignorant character must be allowed to talk the way he talks, but in the author's own exposition.

In *Superior Women,* Alice Adams' sentences have the jerking, lurching feel of a train adding cars in the station. Instead of a cowcatcher, she uses parentheses to scoop up anything that gets in the way:

> Like sexual addicts, which perhaps they are, or very young lovers, which clearly they are not (but perhaps with a kind, late-middle-aged persistence of vision they see each other as young: Jackson as hard-muscled, as taut, and Megan as smoothly voluptuous as when they first met, some thirty-nine years back), all afternoon they made love, in that room.

Adams also gives her sentences little kicks in odd places that send commas flying up into our eyes like cinders:

> "In 1944, there are not many alternatives available, to marriage, for nice young middle-class girls."
> "The most unusual feature of their actually making love, to Megan, is the way Jackson uses his tongue."

"Mid-seat they collide, then, their mouths, arms, breasts, and hands and legs all wildly seeking each other out."

The couple in the last sentence are in a car, so that's what "mid-seat" means, but do men have breasts? Are the alternatives in the first sentence available to marriage or to nice young middle-class girls? Who are the two or more people implied by "their" who are making love to Megan in the second sentence?

Adam's novel was touted as a successor to *The Group*. But there is no reason to eat her heart out, for Mary McCarthy, then, because there is no comparison (absolutely none) at, uh, all.

The need to strike a balance between traditional womanhood and careers by cooking and decorating on paper is one cause of Women's Litter. There are two others.

Feminism's rigidly egalitarian stance has called into question the inherently discriminatory practice of selection demanded by all art. Sometimes the Left seems to be cranking up to a charge of "writism." "Good writing is counter-revolutionary," said Ellen Willis in the *Village Voice*. "Let all the people write," said *Strawberry Statement* author James Simon Kunen. Doubtless they meant well, but the writer *must* function as an elitist, must pick and choose among characters and details, elevating this one and reducing that one, accepting some and rejecting others, all in the name of arbitrary standards. Don't take my word for it; liberal Brigid Brophy said it first: "Art obstinately stands out as the one justifiably aristocratic system, which is reduced to nonsense the instant it abandons the aristocratic principle."

Second, no one wants to write "like men." Many women regard authority in any form as a male trait to be avoided at all cost. Made aware of the way men have controlled them, they no longer feel comfortable with literary control. Being "on top" of the story and characters, keeping everybody and everything in line, being the author-boss, are all reminiscent of male dominance.

But an author is, after all, an authoritarian. The ladies of Women's Litter should exercise their feminist "assertiveness" by adopting the principle of "*Le livre, c'est moi.*"

19

LAND OF HOPEFULLY AND GLORY

If the practitioners of Lockjaw Choctaw in our midst had their way, America's most beloved novel would sound like this:

Scarlett O'Hara was not a physically ideal human being but men seldom perceived it when informed by her life-enhancing qualities as the Tarleton twins were.

"What does it matter if we were expelled from the college of our choice, Scarlett? The hostilities are going to start any any day now. You don't think we'd pursue career-enrichment opportunities with hostilities in progress, do you?"

"Hostilities, hostilities, hostilities! This hostilities dialogue has caveated every party this spring. Besides, there aren't going to be any hostilities."

"Not going to be any hostilities? Why, honey, after the first-strike shelling situation we instituted at Fort Sumter, the Yankees will have to engage in hostilities. Violence always begets violence."

"If you boys don't address another issue, I'll go in the house and express my rage!"

"How about if we tell you a privileged communication? You know Miss Melanie Hamilton who's based in Atlanta? Ashley Wilkes's cousin? They say Ashley's going to marry her. You know the Wilkeses tend to have meaningful relationships with their extended family members."

"Devastating! I'm going to ask Pa if he has any input."

*

"Do you mean to tell me, Katie Scarlett O'Hara, that you neither advocate nor condone home ownership? Why, home ownership is the only viable alternative worth livin' for, worth fightin' for, worth dyin' for, because it's the only comprehensive program for stage-one social mobility."

"Oh, Pa, you talk like a Hibernian-American."

" 'Tis proud I am that I'm Hibernian-American, and don't you be forgettin', Missy, that you're half Hibernian-American, too, and to anyone with a drop of Hibernian blood in him or her, the land he or she lives on is like his or her female parent."

*

"Ashley, I-I love you."

"You musn't say that, Scarlett. It will serve no useful purpose."

"But Ashley, I know you have a felt need for me. Say you have a felt need for me!"

"I have a felt need for you but it has no growth potential. Oh, Scarlett, can't we put a voluntary ban on these things?"

"Don't you want to have a one-on-one commitment with me?"

"I'm going to have a one-on-one commitment with Melanie."

"But you just said you had a felt need for me!"

"I misspoke. My dear, why must you make me verbalize things that will only give you a negative self-image? You're so young and unformulated that you don't know what a one-on-one commitment means."

"I know that I love you."

"Love isn't enough to construct a positive orientation for two people as polarized as we are. You, who are so autonomous and self-realizing—"

"Why don't you articulate it, you wimp? You're threatened by me! You'd rather live with that submissive little nurturer who can't open her mouth except to say 'affirmative' and 'negative,' and parent a network of passive role players just like her!"

"You mustn't say counterproductive things about Melanie. She's part of my gene pool and we interact."

"She's a pale-faced, unassertive ninny and I'm unsupportive of her!"

*

"Miss Scarlett, I don't have no baby-birthin' skills!"

*

"As the Supreme Being is my witness, I'm going to effect a take-charge dynamic with a view toward making it unthinkable that I will ever be inadequately nourished again. I'm going to develop survival techniques, and when it's all over, I'll never be disadvantaged again. If I have to harass, victimize, utilize, or practice situation ethics, I'll never be without my basic nutrients at any subsequent point in time."

*

"Ashley, the Yankees want three hundred dollars to pay the taxes on Tara!"

"Why tell me? You know I can't cope."

FLORENCE KING

"But Ashley, this is a worst-case scenario!"

"What do people do when they're faced with a worst-case scenario? Some are able to initiate direct action to achieve full humanity, while inadequate personalities become victims of the winnowed-out factor."

"Ashley, let's relocate! They need non-combat advisors in the Mexican army. Oh, Ashley, we could have a restructuring experience!"

"I can't leave Melanie. She has no job-training opportunities."

"She has no reproductive capabilities, either, but I could give you—"

"Scarlett, this is totally and categorically unacceptable!"

"Then . . . we have no options?"

"Nothing, except . . . self-esteem."

*

"Rhett, Ashley and I didn't have a meaningful encounter at the lumber yard. We were just building bridges of understanding within a platonic framework."

"Oh, I don't begrudge him recreational sex with you. I can identify with that. Ever since you denied me control over your body, I've reaffirmed myself with surrogates like Belle. But I do begrudge him your consciousness becaue our value judgments are at same-stage. We could have communicated so well, Scarlett, but I couldn't deal with your insecurities so I bonded with Bonnie instead. I'm into fathering now."

*

"Promise me?"

"Anything, Melly."

"Look after Ashley for me. See that he gets counseling, he's so unstructured."

*

"But Rhett, if you leave me, what will I do about re-entry?"

"Frankly, my dear, it doesn't impact me."

194

*

"I'll go home to Tara and monitor the situation. I'll think of some way to re-establish connectedness. After all, tomorrow is another time frame!"

As American *lèse langage* goes, the "less calories than" advertisements really aren't so bad. True degeneration is found in the wordsmithery of small, unknown companies who can't afford to hire the best and the brightest. Operating largely through mail orders, they don't advertise on television or in the major print media. The literature that comes with their products sounds like this:

Congratulations! Your purchase of THE SKID DAISY proves that you are the kind of person that knows what can happen in the bathtub!

THE SKID DAISY obsoletes everything else in bathtub caution.

THE SKID DAISY is different than other safety-oriented devices.

THE SKID DAISY prevents you from a skidding experience as it is designed to totally cover the entire bottom of your bathtub.

THE SKID DAISY allows you to leave go of safety bars and use both hands for your shower activity owing to the fact that it's outer surface is treated with invisible suction cups that gently grip your feet, to the naked eye.

THE SKID DAISY holds your soap still in the event that you dropped it.

THE SKID DAISY decors your whole new bathroom!

THE SKID DAISY gives your guests something to talk about!

That's what THE SKID DAISY is all about!

Directions for installing your THE SKID DAISY:

1. Open bathroom window! Your THE SKID DAISY is treated with a special superchemical which impacts irritating nasal membranes if the room is not air-oriented.

2. Center the drain hole opening over your drain hole and peel away sufficient of it's outer protective layer to expose three or four inches of your THE SKID DAISY to the bottom of your bathtub, pressing.

3. Continue to repeat until your entire bottom of your bathtub is covered and it's outer protective layer is completely peeled off.

4. Feel to see if there are any puckers before wetting it with your fingers.

5. If you are not satisfied with your THE SKID DAISY, write to Pam Parker in our Public Relations Department, or dial 1-800-SKIDNOT, who will address the toll-free problem.

Do not write to Pam Parker unless you want more of the same, because she and the classical stylist who wrote the brochure are one and the same person:

> Dear Ms. King:
>
> Firstly, let me say how sorry we were to hear about your experience with regard to your THE SKID DAISY.
>
> Thank you muchly for the X-ray of your irritating membranes, the photograph of your bathtub, the photograph of your feet, and the other photograph. With this end in view, I have transpired it to our lawyer's, who will formulate an irrespective opinion as to the obligation of your injuries, pertaining.
>
> As you wrote to us previous to the time limit within 30 days of the subsequent purchase agreement to the dead line's running out was up, our

warranty gladly inforces us a guarantee to send you a free gift replacement of a new THE SKID DAISY.

Please advise as to which choice you wish to prefer between the Greek Temples, Tropical Paradise, Arizona Sunset, or our new Chinese-oriented design.

Skidlessly Your's,
Pam

20 EPILOGUE

I've sung of strangers seeking class,
Full of smiling fury,
Wandering lonely as a cloud
And serving on a jury.

So it's home again, and home again,
America for me!
Where they punch you out for smoking
And not saying "he or she."
The land of giddy voters
Where all have got the right
To step into the booth and cast
A certain slant of blight.

It takes a heap o' heapin'
In a house to make a heap
Of women's liberation
That would make a strong man weep.
Of Crisis Outreach Hot Lines
And a host of working mothers,
And constant admonitions
To be sensitive to others.

Regarding our Democrazy
And all of those who love it,
I'll quote my angel mother now
And end by saying "Shove it."